go get 'em!
Larry

D O L

# FLASHPOINTS
## for achievers

this daily journal is presented to

D1473584

_____

because I believe in the powerful combination of
inspiration, knowledge, service and action.

_____

**other books by larrybroughton:**

VICTORY: 7 Entrepreneurial Success Strategies for Veterans
(with Phil Dyer)

Tenacity

## praise for flashpoints for achievers

*"FLASHPOINTS for achievers" is fresh, poignant and uniquely insightful. The messages never fail to cause me to pause, take note and consider how each point can make me better at what I do.*
**DARREN HARDY, PUBLISHER OF** *SUCCESS MAGAZINE;*
**New York Times best-selling author of** *The Compound Effect*

*FLASHPOINTS deliver messages that inspire me and are usually just what I needed to hear. They never fail to bring me clarity and put me in a more positive frame of mind.*
**RON OGULNICK**
**Ogulnick, Leventhal, Cajka, LLP**

*We all live busy, complicated lives. Sometimes the hardest thing is to simplify, to pare down all the clutter and invest our time and energy in the right things at the right time. FLASHPOINTS have become an anchor for me as I strive to become the best professional, husband and father I can be. Larry's insights have enriched my thinking, and offer valuable, ongoing perspective as I negotiate all the "stuff" that makes up daily living.*
**CURT MCCORMICK**
**Director, Corporate Communications and Public Relations**
**MedStar Health, Columbia, MD**

*Larry Broughton's FLASHPOINTS offer nourishment for achievers who are hungry for a shift in their thinking about significance in business and life. Each thought-provoking message inspires reflection on how great we are, and how amazing we can become.*
**CHIP CONLEY**
**Founder, Joie de Vivre Hotels;**
**New York Times best-selling author of** *Emotional Equations* **and** *Peak*

*Succinct...Poignant...Fresh thinking...FLASHPOINTS add a bright spot to my day, and set me in the right direction.*
**BRUCE DINGMAN, PRESIDENT**
**The Dingman Company, Inc.**

I always look forward to the opportunity to view and absorb the touch & feel of FLASHPOINTS. Too often these subtle reminders of the do's and don'ts of common sense and courtesy are overlooked or purposely avoided. Their synopsis reminds one to focus on what should be the norm and mantra of sensibility and common courtesy. To follow these premises should undoubtedly help build or rebuild character and make the recipient a better person, personally and professionally.

**IRWIN WOLDMAN**
**Marcus Millichap**


I look forward to my time reflecting on FLASHPOINTS as they are always worth reading, often worth saving and sharing - with colleagues certainly, but with my family too, at the dinner table where they are the starting point of lively and important discussions. I am able to introduce many topics that might otherwise fall on deaf or unreceptive ears - especially those of my teen-age son. Knowing a little of Larry's many accomplishments, my son, who aspires to attend one of the military academies, is more likely to take my advice when I can cite as laudable a source as Big Larry for confirmation.

**BEVERLY HELD, DIRECTOR**
**SF Seminars**


There seem to be an infinite number of self-proclaimed experts offering tips, quotes and thoughts of the day, but when it comes to quality insight in business and life, there are none that even make the entrance ramp to the caliber of FLASHPOINTS. The very depth of Larry Broughton comes through in each message, making one wonder…does he write or channel them?

**ROBERTA ROSS**
**President, Six Figure Real Estate Coach, Inc.**
**"America's Real Estate Lead Generation Expert"**


Larry's daily dose of FLASHPOINTS offers clarity, insight and guidance for leaders and achievers. Each message will enlighten and inspire you to transform your team, your business, and your life.

**BRIAN TRACY**
**CEO, Brian Tracy International;**
**International best-selling author and keynote speaker**

# FLASHPOINTS

## for achievers

*inspiring messages that bring significant results*

a daily journal

**larrybroughton**

FLASHPOINTS for achievers: inspiring messages that bring significant results, a daily journal
By Larry Broughton

Published by Bandera Publishing, 2400 E. Katella Ave, Suite 300, Anaheim, California, 92806, www.BanderaPublishing.com

Excerpts from this book have been previously published by Larry Broughton in 2010, 2011, 2012, and 2013.

www.FLASHPOINTSdaily.com

Broughton, Larry

## this journal is dedicated to

my two favorite people in the world: my daughter, Emmy, whose creativity, compassion and tenacity inspires me and everyone she touches; and my son, Bullet, whose positive attitude, adventurous spirit and sense of humor brings joy to my life. These two blessings are the greatest of the many gifts God has bestowed on me.

# FLASHPOINTS
## resources

For information on our FLASHPOINTS Podcast, and for more tools to assist you on your FLASHPOINTS journey, please visit
**FLASHPOINTSdaily.com**

---

### multiple copies
If you would like to order 5 or more copies of FLASHPOINTS daily journal, please contact us at
**bookorder@FLASHPOINTSdaily.com**

---

### keynotes
To have Larry Broughton speak at your event or organization about leadership, elite team building, strategic vision, entrepreneurship, or the principles found in FLASHPOINTS for achievers, email
**speaker@FLASHPOINTSdaily.com**

---

### bonuses
Thank you for joining our FLASHPOINTS tribe by purchasing this book. For a list of Thank You bonuses, please visit
**FLASHPOINTSdaily.com/bookbonuses**

## about larrybroughton

Larry is an award-winning entrepreneur & CEO, best-selling author, keynote speaker, mentor, screw-up and failure, and a man on a mission to transform his life and the lives of entrepreneurs and achievers around the globe. After growing up in a small mill town in rural western New York, he spent eight years traveling the world with the US Army's elite Special Forces, commonly known as the Green Berets.

Larry has successfully parlayed his unique experience of serving on Special Forces A-Teams to the business arena. He is Founder/CEO of broughtonHOTELS, a leader in the boutique hotel industry; and Co-Founder/CEO of BROUGHTONadvisory a strategic vision, elite team building, and transformational leadership organization with clients ranging from entrepreneurial start-ups to Turner Broadcasting and The Pentagon. He's received numerous awards for business performance, innovation and leadership; including Ernst & Young's prestigious *Entrepreneur of the Year®* , NaVOBA'S (National Veteran-Owned Business Association) *Vetrepreneur® of the Year,* Coastline Foundation's *Visionary of the Year,* and Passkeys Foundation's *Business Leader of Integrity,* while *Entrepreneur Magazine* included broughtonHOTELS in their *Hot 500* List.

Larry lives and works in Orange County, CA; and is blessed with a beautiful daughter, Emily; and dashing son, Ben. Dedicated to life-long learning, he has interviewed hundreds of successful entrepreneurs, CEOs and thought leaders on the topics of business, leadership, entrepreneurship and significance. Larry has attended the Executive Program at prestigious Stanford University; studied Russian at the world- renowned Defense Language Institute; and studied Political Science at University of California, Santa Barbara and College of San Mateo.

Learn more and follow Larry at:

facebook.com/larry.broughton

twitter.com/larrybroughton

linkedin.com/in/larrybroughton

aboutLARRYbroughton.com

BROUGHTONadvisory.com

broughtonHOTELS.com

# acknowledgments

This book was not an accident! It was years in the making (as I explain in the introduction), with a big push to get us over the finish line.

Although inspired by many, I need to acknowledge a few folks who have made a significant impact on this project.

Thanks to Dean Del Sesto who helped launch my weekly FLASHPOINTS five years ago; whose insights and writings during that first year laid the ground work for me to expand the mission and audience from just a few hundred weekly readers, to tens of thousands who are now regularly impacted by FLASHPOINTS.

Thanks to Darren Hardy, Publisher of SUCCESS Magazine, who encouraged me three years ago to get FLASHPOINTS into a book format; and for offering his kind words as a testimonial to the power of FLASHPOINTS.

Thanks to my dear friends Darrell Fusaro and Marcus Slaton; both of whom have encouraged me to accept who God made me to be, and prodded me to let go of the demons that haunted me; offered reminders to simply bless others; and stood by me during some of the darkest moments of my life.

A very special thank you to our rock star graphic designer, Chris Pineda, who (under tight deadlines) jumped through hoops to make the feel and flow of this book visually appealing and easy on the eye. I am grateful to Christine Stossel who offered feedback when entries did not make sense, and whose editing efforts and eye for detail made this journal eminently more readable.

Thanks to Dave Braun, my friend and FLASHPOINTSdaily.com partner. He's an encourager, arranger and visionary who saw the power of FLASHPOINTS, and stepped up to get this important project across the finish line.

If you are a friend, family member, or co-worker I've not mentioned here, take heart; whether you know it or not, you've inspired one or more of the entries in this book, as each one comes from a daily lesson learned on my recent journey.

# CAUTION!

Don't be fooled by the simple format of this daily journal. Entrepreneurs, CEOs and super achievers from across the U.S. and Canada have shared their stories of the transformational power of the poignant messages found in these pages.

Take note: daily reading and reflecting on FLASHPOINTS messages will certainly ignite the spark of internal change, but real transformation only comes from applying the lessons learned by taking rapid action, and being tenacious in your pursuit of living a life of service and significance.

# intro & how to use this journal

For nearly five years I've been providing weekly tidbits of inspiration and wisdom to a growing tribe of FLASHPOINTS followers...many of whom offer regular feedback on how a particular message has moved them, or ignited their spirit to take action towards their dreams.

As I've traveled around the country in recent years, I've been impressed to learn how entrepreneurs, CEOs, athletes, politicians and leaders have used my weekly FLASHPOINTS to inspire personal and professional growth; and as a training tool for staff meetings and team member development. I've heard from many FLASHPOINTS readers that they regularly post the messages on bulletin boards, or in prominent locations above their desks...and they've often shared how they'd like to see the weekly email messages more frequently, or have them printed in a journal format. Well, we've taken those requests and turned it up a notch or two.

In addition to including weekly FLASHPOINTS in the email blasts that I send out for BROUGHTONadvisory, the daily journal you're holding offers a different FLASHPOINTS message each Monday through Friday, with a daily Reflections and Intentions section of thought-provoking questions to help us find mental and emotional clarity. Each week is wrapped up with Weekly Reflections on Saturday, while each week is launched with a Weekly Intentions for goal setting each Sunday. Feel free to jot down your thoughts related to the daily message, but take note that there are no lines on which to write your answers to the questions.

Those who grew up with me may get a good chuckle out of this, but I like to think of myself as fairly articulate. There are, however, days when I can't put my own thoughts and feelings into coherent sentences; but I am able to scratch out one bold word with an over-exaggerated exclamation point, or sketch a quick picture or draw a stick figure of the person I'm thinking of. With that in mind, we've resisted placing boundaries on you by leaving some open space on each page for your doodles. Be creative...have fun!

Addicted to forward motion and achievement most of my life, I've found more personal and professional growth during the past two and one-half years than any other season of my life. Perhaps you've heard me talk about the transformational power I've found in my seven-minute morning routine. Introduced to me by my friend and mentor, Darrell Fusaro, each day (before checking email, social media sites, shaving, showering, or turning on the morning news), I spend seven minutes with my veggie smoothie (or cup of coffee), doing some meditations, prayers and inspirational reading in order to set my daily intentions for good; and to focus my mind and spirit on the right path for each day. Left to my own devices, I find myself pushing and shoving to the proverbial front of the line for my share of "success"...which in the end, always feels empty. As Darrell often reminds me, "if you have to fight for what you want, you have to fight to keep it...and that gets tiring."

cont.

I'm grateful he shared this wisdom and technique with me, as my seven-minute routine has become the single most powerful and impactful tool in my arsenal for achievement. With it's insightful readings and inspiring messages, it sometimes turns into fifteen or twenty minutes and reminds me of the important topics of the day (and often offers new insights from others who have walked the path before me).

Knowing the power that comes from starting each day with a morning routine and emotional tune-up, I've been humbled and inspired by those who have shared with me how they've incorporated FLASHPOINTS into their own daily routines. So, with your new FLASHPOINTS for achievers daily journal in hand, I encourage you to find a comfortable place in your home to start each day with a moment of meditation, prayer and reading. After reading the corresponding FLASHPOINTS, record your reflections and intentions in the daily journal, and revisit your morning thoughts throughout the day to stay on track.

There are a couple of ways to use this powerful journal: First, you can just start at the beginning of the journal with "week 1" (no matter the week of the year), and reflect on the corresponding day's FLASHPOINTS, and record your reflections and intentions on each page. Be sure to give yourself 30 days to form a routine; but if you skip a few days from time-to-time throughout the year don't fret, just pick it up again, and continue on the journey.

The second, and most powerful way to use this journal is to identify the week of the calendar year we're in, and read the corresponding day's FLASHPOINTS. Since we're all built for community, you can take heart that thousands of fellow achievement seekers around the country will be reflecting on the same message each day along with you. We're on this journey together. If you need help identifying which week we're in during the calendar year, simply visit FLASHPOINTSdaily.com for a countdown calendar at the top of the page.

Since none of us can find enduring significance in life as a lone wolf, I'll be on the achievement journey with you... reading and reflecting on the same daily message as the rest of the FLASHPOINTS tribe. Because I get a kick out of inspiring others, and one of my personal goals is to live a life of authenticity and transparency, I'll be providing a weekly podcast where I'll share my victories, disappointments, challenges, and lessons each week. I'll let you know what worked, and what didn't; what I've learned and how I plan to improve. You can learn more about my FLASHPOINTS Podcast at FLASHPOINTSdaily.com.

Thanks again for joining us on this exciting journey, and for being a member of the FLASHPOINTS tribe. I'd love to hear your comments and stories about how a particular daily messages may have resonated with you, and how your achievement journey is being impacted by FLASHPOINTS. Please send me your insights at feedback@FLASHPOINTSdaily.com.

## Communication is an exchange of ideas, both verbal and nonverbal.

Gone is the day when a command and control leadership style of barking orders in a morning meeting effectively directs workflow for the day. Long gone is the day when being a good manager meant always having the right answer. We simply can't do it alone! Inspiring those around us to become proactive, critical thinkers and independent leaders means we must involve them in the creative and problem-solving process. Remember, though, effective communication is a two-way street. To create and sustain significant change, it's important to listen. It sounds easy, but *listening* is much more than just *hearing* what people say. Can you sense their stress, loss of motivation, and feelings of purpose, excitement, disappointment, and fear—even when they're not spoken aloud? *How can you hear less and listen more?*

## reflections and intentions

my thoughts and feelings on today's FLASHPOINTS include:

my intentions and action items today include:

today I am grateful for:

## The pursuit of our passions requires inspiration and courage ... and is our path to greatness.

I often write about following our passion, committing to serving others, and seeking significance to achieve super-charged results. But, what happens when we can't quite identify or articulate our passions? Keep in mind that everything new or outside our inherent strengths will seem like hard work ... whether we're passionate or not. Discovering our passions, however, requires reflection and exploration. So, get out! Travel, volunteer, serve others, and push the boundaries a bit. Think about the things you enjoy doing when you aren't working: What gets you excited? What do you like to read and learn about? With whom do you surround yourself? Where do you like to be? Among these exercise and exploits we'll likely find our ticket to a more meaningful existence. *Is your path to greatness paved with passion?*

### reflections and intentions

my thoughts and feelings on today's FLASHPOINTS include:

my intentions and action items today include:

today I am grateful for:

# All good things begin as a daydream.

Every innovation, romance, discovery and adventure began as the fantasy of an optimistic daydreamer. I once heard that we should be focusing our energy and resources on those things we think about when we daydream (or what we do when we're procrastinating). Let your mind wander around that one for a minute! For some people this simply means spending more time doing what we love or getting intentional about our bucket list; for others, it means a long overdue career change. Ouch! How honest are you with yourself about what excites you? Although a simple question, it can be difficult to answer because it takes courage to give ourselves permission to dream big. Schedule time to daydream, and note where your mind wanders. *Where's your mind taking you today?*

## reflections and intentions

my thoughts and feelings on today's FLASHPOINTS include:

my intentions and action items today include:

today I am grateful for:

## When you find someone who inspires you to be a better person, let them know and never let them go!

Authenticity and genuine leadership rarely intersect, so it's tough to identify role models who excite us and cause us to reach for our fullest potential. Whereas mentors can be found in the writings and recordings of those long since passed, the rules for this scenario are they must be alive, contactable, and worthy of emulation! Personally, I find it difficult to find all the great traits that inspire me wrapped up in one person, so I admire specific traits in specific people. When we admire someone, we must let them know ... don't keep that gift of encouragement to yourself. Sometimes a simple word of thanks can fuel the next great breakthrough. Everyone needs a cheerleader, even our heroes and role models. *Who inspires you to greatness? Tell them that!*

## reflections and intentions

my thoughts and feelings on today's FLASHPOINTS include:

my intentions and action items today include:

today I am grateful for:

# Time.
## It's what we long for most, but leverage the least.

At the core of so many discussions is this familiar refrain: "I wish I had more time!" Really? Do you really think you'd have a better grasp on your life if you had a longer day, or would you simply stuff those bonus hours full of more mundane to-dos? Perhaps more hours in the day isn't the right way to look at it. How about setting more realistic timeframes and deploying the appropriate resources to reach the goals to begin with? Smarter still, we must surround ourselves with higher-functioning teammates to help get more done (with less). Or consider an overhaul of our systems—maybe there are ways to save time, talent and resources. *How can you stuff greater results (not tasks) into your tomorrow?*

## reflections and intentions

my thoughts and feelings on today's FLASHPOINTS include:

my intentions and action items today include:

today I am grateful for:

# STOP!

**to maximize your FLASHPOINTS experience:**

1. turn to page XV and read *introduction and how to use this journal*

2. visit FLASHPOINTSdaily.com/bookbonuses for extra free resources

3. subscribe to "FLASHPOINTS for achievers podcast" (see website for details)

> ## The bad news is time flies. The good news is you're the pilot.
> ~ Michael Altshuler

After five days of prompting and prodding new ideas and thoughts to come to mind, today we review what we've discovered. It's time to take a peek back at our journaling, to review our thoughts, feelings, and action items; and see how well we did. After all, self-awareness is the key to initiate growth and realize lasting change.

## weekly reflection

reflecting on my thoughts, feelings and experiences from this past week, the top three that impacted me the most include:

my top "ta-da's" (successes) from this past week include:

my top "oh-no's" (disappointments) from this past week include:

my top "ah-ha's" (discoveries) from this past week include:

> # Some of us learn from other people's mistakes and the rest of us have to be other people.
>
> ### ~ Zig Ziglar

The end of the week is the best time to plan for the coming week. And at this point, you've reviewed the previous week and can be prepared to make changes and take actions based on thought, not re-action. You want to keep your goals in mind always. So today is your opportunity to look at yesterday's Weekly Reflection and decide what you're going to do and when. It is most often small tweaks that will lead to great success, fueled by a positive and grateful attitude.

## weekly intentions

my top "go get-'em's" (fixes) to implement this coming week include:

incomplete action items, that support my goals, to carry over into this coming week include: (schedule them now and be specific.)

new action items, that support my goals, for this coming week include: (schedule them now and be specific.)

something new I'm grateful for this week, and with whom I will share it:

## All work and no play makes Jack a dull boy.

Most of us spend more time at work than doing anything else; it's no wonder some of our most significant friendships are with people at work. At one extreme, these friendships lead to distractions or too much of a relaxed environment; at the other extreme, nurturing these friendships produces benefits such as team cohesion, increased trust and focus on the mission. To gently foster unit cohesion and team spirit, how about a weekly lunch, or moving the Friday night drinks to Wednesday for a mid-week boost, or introducing a monthly service project to help assist others in need? Work some conversation and fun into your team's schedule, so it isn't missed during work hours. You'll be surprised how the smiles and productivity skyrocket! *What will you do for play today?*

## reflections and intentions

my thoughts and feelings on today's FLASHPOINTS include:

my intentions and action items today include:

today I am grateful for:

# Dang!
# Why didn't I think of that?

In virtually every area of life, success is often defined by innovation. While some ideas may come to us in the shower, those at the cutting edge know it's important to build their clutter-free days around dreaming, trying new things, and generating new ideas. When it comes to ideation and creation, it's really no coincidence that someone beat us to the finish line. Simply put—they thought of it first because they set out to do so. If we want to find our next big idea, we can't wait for it to magically appear while lathering up in the shower. Schedule brainstorming and creative open space into the calendar each week and ask provocative questions about systems, services and products. *What will you start doing today to allow for innovation?*

## reflections and intentions

my thoughts and feelings on today's FLASHPOINTS include:

my intentions and action items today include:

today I am grateful for:

# Artistic manifestations are often considered the truest form of self-expression. So, too, is achievement and leadership.

There are self-doubters and downers who don't consider their own efforts legitimate until their craft is paying the bills. Similarly, there are those leaders and achievers who don't see the significance of their successes as much more than impressive feats to list on a resume. *Stop doing that!* The critical roles we play have a positive and direct impact on the health of our communities and shouldn't be treated as hobbies. The valuable services we provide our spheres of influence can change lives and should serve as a significant form of self-expression. This realization occurs when we stop making things all about us and start making it about serving others. *How would your self-expression and choices be made if they were based on serving others?*

## reflections and intentions

my thoughts and feelings on today's FLASHPOINTS include:

my intentions and action items today include:

today I am grateful for:

## Do you know where you're going to?

You can't book a vacation without first deciding where you're off to, right? Similarly, in life, it helps to have a clearly defined vision of our dreams and destination in order to plan the trip. Where do you want your journey to take you? When do you want to arrive? Start with the ending point in mind and work backward. Like any adventure that begins as an easy jaunt, excitement and growth often come from the unexpected detours along the way. What do you hope to achieve within 10 years, 5 years, 2 years, 1 year, and in the next 6 months? Taking the time to map out our strategy is a fundamental part of achieving our vision. *So what are you waiting for? Get mapping now!*

## reflections and intentions

my thoughts and feelings on today's FLASHPOINTS include:

my intentions and action items today include:

today I am grateful for:

# Facts can be finagled, but authenticity can't be faked.

It's bolder than religion or pop culture, bigger than the latest breaking world news, and better than the release of Apple's latest iProduct! I'm talking about the power of presenting our authentic, true selves to the world. Although it's often the most challenging and painful events in life that ignite our spark of authenticity and transparency, the journey usually leads to our most significant season of joy, freedom and connectedness. Most of us are afraid that if others *really* know us for who we *really* are, they'd run the other way. Yet, it's the alignment of head and heart, thinking and saying, feeling and doing, that others find most attractive about us. Authenticity builds trust, and followers love leaders they trust. *How can you stretch and be more authentic today?*

## reflections and intentions

my thoughts and feelings on today's FLASHPOINTS include:

my intentions and action items today include:

today I am grateful for:

> # *Half of being smart is knowing what you are dumb about.*
>
> ## ~ Solomon Short

After five days of prompting and prodding new ideas and thoughts to come to mind, today we review what we've discovered. It's time to take a peek back at our journaling, to review our thoughts, feelings, and action items; and see how well we did. After all, self-awareness is the key to initiate growth and realize lasting change.

## weekly reflection

reflecting on my thoughts, feelings and experiences from this past week, the top three that impacted me the most include:

my top "ta-da's" (successes) from this past week include:

my top "oh-no's" (disappointments) from this past week include:

my top "ah-ha's" (discoveries) from this past week include:

> ## *If you're doing something the same way you have been doing it for ten years, the chances are you are doing it wrong.*
> ~ Charles Kettering

The end of the week is the best time to plan for the coming week. And at this point, you've reviewed the previous week and can be prepared to make changes and take actions based on thought, not re-action. You want to keep your goals in mind always. So today is your opportunity to look at yesterday's Weekly Reflection and decide what you're going to do and when. It is most often small tweaks that will lead to great success, fueled by a positive and grateful attitude.

## weekly intentions

my top "go get-'em's" (fixes) to implement this coming week include:

incomplete action items, that support my goals, to carry over into this coming week include: (schedule them now and be specific.)

new action items, that support my goals, for this coming week include: (schedule them now and be specific.)

something new I'm grateful for this week, and with whom I will share it:

## Sharing is caring.
## Mentoring is molding.

Mentors aren't just for entrepreneurs or business people any longer. Everyone can learn from others who have "been there and done that." It wasn't long ago when mentors became recognized as important assets for emerging entrepreneurs and small business owners. Until then, only serious, career-minded executives and big-league business owners even considered this luxury. If forced to pick just one strategy or tool to help find success in any endeavor, it would be having a mentor (or several). Who isn't keen on a more abundant, joyful and high-impact existence? The truth is, we all strive for a more successful and significant life... whatever that might mean to each of us. *Open your mind to your greatest possibilities and reach your fullest potential: In what mentoring relationship can you be engaged?*

## reflections and intentions

my thoughts and feelings on today's FLASHPOINTS include:

my intentions and action items today include:

today I am grateful for:

# Magic happens when things get done that we don't want to do.

We all have those few insignificant tasks that seem to stay on our to-do lists forever. They drop to the bottom of the list and then just linger. While there's nothing wrong with a to-do list, these ever-present tasks can zap our mental energy, prevent us from finding clarity and hold us back from reaching our fullest potential. If we really want significant breakthroughs, here's the challenge: start from the bottom of that to-do list today and honestly assess why those tasks haven't yet been tackled. Do they require strengths, skills and talents that lay outside our comfort zone? If so, delete them from that list, delegate them to another team member, or defer them to another time. *What's on your to-do list that you can delete, delegate, or defer?*

## reflections and intentions

my thoughts and feelings on today's FLASHPOINTS include:

my intentions and action items today include:

today I am grateful for:

# Leaders are defined by the achievements of their team, not the details of their daily decisions.

Sometimes a leader's role is not to lead, but rather to be a mirror. Consider that the highest functioning, most elite team doesn't need a leader to micromanage or make daily decisions at all. It requires a leader who can ask profound questions and identify the needs of the unit, then remove the bureaucratic barriers so they can defy the odds and accomplish their mission. We must ask ourselves whether we're controlling, enabling, or enhancing our team's effectiveness. Here's a quick test: If we walked away from our team, would it continue to function successfully without us? If not, perhaps it's time to consider cutting back on our decision-making and control and encourage them to self-delegate and problem solve among themselves. *To what level are you serving or suffocating your team?*

## reflections and intentions

my thoughts and feelings on today's FLASHPOINTS include:

my intentions and action items today include:

today I am grateful for:

# Like lipstick on a pig, procrastination is really just fear with a fancy title.

Can you recall a fearful time in your life, when you fought the fright and accomplished the goal? *It felt awesome,* right? For most of us, the next thought was, "Why did I take so long to do that?" Fear. Fear of making a mistake, of taking longer than expected, of looking like a fool, of change, of results not meeting expectations. Listen, it's okay to procrastinate—briefly— but self-awareness is vital to understanding the difference between not being ready and fear. So, how do we give fear the middle finger? Take *action!* One small step ... then another ... and soon you'll have an indescribable view from the top of a mountain, looking out over your accomplishments. Start climbing! *What will you do today that'll get you closer to your goal?*

## reflections and intentions

my thoughts and feelings on today's FLASHPOINTS include:

my intentions and action items today include:

today I am grateful for:

## You've heard, "Find a Why that will make you Cry." You need to re-think that RIGHT NOW!

I've read countless self-help and personal development books. Most talk about finding a *"Why"* that's truly heart-centered, moving and important. That's helpful but only partially correct; they stop at finding a *"Why that will make us Cry."* That's not good enough! We're competing against a rising global economy where people are willing to fight (and fight hard) to grow their market share and influence. But what IS good enough? Do this: Find a Why that will make you *DIE!* Shocking? It shouldn't be. Think of those who've achieved the most lasting, significant global impact: Gandhi, Jesus, Martin Luther King, Mother Teresa, our Armed Forces ... while some are willing to die physically, all have died to themselves! Now answer this life-altering question: *What's your Why that will make you DIE?*

### reflections and intentions

my thoughts and feelings on today's FLASHPOINTS include:

my intentions and action items today include:

today I am grateful for:

> ## We must all suffer from one of two pains: the pain of discipline or the pain of regret. The difference is discipline weighs ounces while regret weighs tons.
> ~ Jim Rohn

After five days of prompting and prodding new ideas and thoughts to come to mind, today we review what we've discovered. It's time to take a peek back at our journaling, to review our thoughts, feelings, and action items; and see how well we did. After all, self-awareness is the key to initiate growth and realize lasting change.

## weekly reflection

reflecting on my thoughts, feelings and experiences from this past week, the top three that impacted me the most include:

my top "ta-da's" (successes) from this past week include:

my top "oh-no's" (disappointments) from this past week include:

my top "ah-ha's" (discoveries) from this past week include:

> # We must look for the opportunity in every difficulty instead of being paralyzed at the thought of the difficulty in every opportunity.
> ~ Walter E. Cole

The end of the week is the best time to plan for the coming week. And at this point, you've reviewed the previous week and can be prepared to make changes and take actions based on thought, not re-action. You want to keep your goals in mind always. So today is your opportunity to look at yesterday's Weekly Reflection and decide what you're going to do and when. It is most often small tweaks that will lead to great success, fueled by a positive and grateful attitude.

## weekly intentions

my top "go get-'em's" (fixes) to implement this coming week include:

incomplete action items, that support my goals, to carry over into this coming week include: (schedule them now and be specific.)

new action items, that support my goals, for this coming week include: (schedule them now and be specific.)

something new I'm grateful for this week, and with whom I will share it:

> ## Miracles begin when we place as much energy and action in reaching our dreams as we do in avoiding our fears.

Picture this! <<Enter your ultimate life fantasy here.>> We have the ability to dream up insanely satisfying fantasies of our ideal life. Most of us fail, however, to take decisive action toward making those dreams reality. So, too often, those dreams remain just a pretty picture in our minds. Some high achievers go to the next step and develop vision boards, with pasted images of their ideal life as inspiration and reminders of their ultimate prize. They hang their boards in their office or family rooms to inspire them toward their goals. Without taking action, however, a vision board is just another pretty collage. Whatever our excuse for not realizing our dreams, it's usually just *us* standing in our own way. *What roadblocks are preventing you from taking action today?*

## reflections and intentions

my thoughts and feelings on today's FLASHPOINTS include:

my intentions and action items today include:

today I am grateful for:

## Your community needs you.
## But which *you* do they need?

Answer: The *transformed* you. You're designed with an ambition to enhance your own life and the lives of those around you. True transformation simply starts with a decision—*your* decision. But what's next? Try these four steps: 1. Forgive—let go of any resentment, *especially toward yourself.* 2. Stop spending time exclusively on the urgent—get off the treadmill briefly and decide what's truly important. 3. Break away from the current you—do something you've always wanted. 4. Clean up a mess—you need to make room so the new can come into your life. *When are you going to start unleashing your true power? The world needs it to be TODAY!*

## reflections and intentions

my thoughts and feelings on today's FLASHPOINTS include:

my intentions and action items today include:

today I am grateful for:

## Self-improvement rarely works without seasoned role models who bring out the hope pent up inside ourselves.

Have you heard that "you don't know what you don't know?" Well, we do know that there's always more to learn. Every super achiever admits that they're dedicated to learning, so they surround themselves with positive influences, and they seek the company of like-minded people who have traveled the path before them. Isn't that what mentoring relationships are all about? Think of someone whose accomplishments resemble your goals at the summit of your journey. Reach out to them; they'll likely humbled by your request to begin a mentoring relationship. What's the lifetime value of one good idea? Isn't it worth the investment of time and capital to shallow your learning curve with the help of a mentor? *When will you make the call?*

## reflections and intentions

my thoughts and feelings on today's FLASHPOINTS include:

my intentions and action items today include:

today I am grateful for:

## It's not their, it's they're.
## It's not your, it's you're.

It's not the spelling that's important, but what it says about us that's important. In a fiercely competitive business environment, attention to quality and detail sets us apart from the crowd. Our language communicates the kind of leader and businessperson we aspire to be. But what's your language saying about you? If our words get sloppy, customers, clients and investors may begin to think the same of our other business practices. And if we're allowing poor language to slide by in the workplace, then what comes next? Let's set a standard for our teams and ourselves by putting our best foot forward at every opportunity. Words have power. Words have meaning. They do, after all, attract others to us. *How can you improve your words to be more attractive?*

## reflections and intentions

my thoughts and feelings on today's FLASHPOINTS include:

my intentions and action items today include:

today I am grateful for:

## Achievement should be less like life and death and more like fun and games.

Our road to success need not be paved with furrowed brows and clenched teeth. We've created (or become part of) a team because we know it will leverage our ideas, talents and resources for greater impact, right? Team morale, productivity, and engagement increase when we have a playful spirit and have fun. So, it's our priority to serve our team, fuel their creativity, and ensure they're enjoying the ride. No matter our title, from time to time, we all need to act as CFO (that's Chief FUN Officer)! Although our cause may be a serious one, we can still ensure our team members, and we ourselves, have opportunities to socialize, communicate, and have some good old-fashioned fun along the way. *How much fun are you and your team having today?*

## reflections and intentions

my thoughts and feelings on today's FLASHPOINTS include:

my intentions and action items today include:

today I am grateful for:

> # Leadership is an opportunity to serve. It is not a trumpet call to self-importance.
> ### ~ J. Donald Walters

After five days of prompting and prodding new ideas and thoughts to come to mind, today we review what we've discovered. It's time to take a peek back at our journaling, to review our thoughts, feelings, and action items; and see how well we did. After all, self-awareness is the key to initiate growth and realize lasting change.

## weekly reflection

reflecting on my thoughts, feelings and experiences from this past week, the top three that impacted me the most include:

my top "ta-da's" (successes) from this past week include:

my top "oh-no's" (disappointments) from this past week include:

my top "ah-ha's" (discoveries) from this past week include:

> ## *A man learns to skate by staggering about making a fool of himself; indeed, he progresses in all things by making a fool of himself.*
>
> ~ George Bernard Shaw

The end of the week is the best time to plan for the coming week. And at this point, you've reviewed the previous week and can be prepared to make changes and take actions based on thought, not re-action. You want to keep your goals in mind always. So today is your opportunity to look at yesterday's Weekly Reflection and decide what you're going to do and when. It is most often small tweaks that will lead to great success, fueled by a positive and grateful attitude.

## weekly intentions

my top "go get-'em's" (fixes) to implement this coming week include:

incomplete action items, that support my goals, to carry over into this coming week include: (schedule them now and be specific.)

new action items, that support my goals, for this coming week include: (schedule them now and be specific.)

something new I'm grateful for this week, and with whom I will share it:

## Like a poker player with a handful of aces, you've got the goods! It's time to go all in.

Too many of us wait too long to launch that new project, new business, or new us. We rationalize and dramatize our past decisions and shortcomings so much, that we ask for a clean slate to start over by way of New Year's resolutions. But without fierce commitment and follow up, we're usually back where we started by February. Why? Because we've not yet made the most important choice: *to go all in*. Without the proclamation to risk it all and give our goals a *real* shot, we don't stand a chance to realize long-term success. Going all in means doing whatever it takes, and persevering until we've won the pot. *What goal has been eluding you? Is it time you went all in?*

## reflections and intentions

my thoughts and feelings on today's FLASHPOINTS include:

my intentions and action items today include:

today I am grateful for:

# God did His job by giving us life; it's our job to start living.

Here's a news flash: we have but one life to live. That's it, sorry! Since most folks already know that, why do so many of us have such major regrets as we approach the end of life? Well, because we get caught up just *surviving*, and not *thriving* ... which is actually living. Break free from that suffocating survival mode by asking yourself: *If this were my last day on earth, how would I look back on my life?* Write down three things that would cause you to feel you've really lived. Perhaps it's spending quality time with family, serving hurting people, starting that business or taking that dream vacation. Don't delay! Whatever it is, make plans *now* to do it before it's too late. *Stop surviving and start LIVING!*

## reflections and intentions

my thoughts and feelings on today's FLASHPOINTS include:

my intentions and action items today include:

today I am grateful for:

## If we don't know the destination, we won't recognize when we're off course.

Having vision is about imagining the possibility of what could be. Perhaps it's launching a world-changing organization or a successful career or developing an innovative new product. The list is endless, and it's as unique as we are. For many of us, it feels like a lifetime effort to realize our vision. It's often difficult to stay focused, maintain our stamina and remain patient, as goals and visions of greatness are usually the most elusive. Sometimes, those voices in our heads (and of family and friends) become like a child on a long road trip asking, "Are we there yet?" When patience seems to be running thin, we must take a deep breath and remember where we're going. *How clear is your mental picture of your destination?*

### reflections and intentions

my thoughts and feelings on today's FLASHPOINTS include:

my intentions and action items today include:

today I am grateful for:

# When the going gets tough ... give thanks.

When times are tough, it's easy to focus on the negative. When we're in the dumps, it's as though we're viewing the world through a pair of goggles that only makes the ugly stuff visible. So, take off those goggles! Focus on the positives to pull yourself out of that slump ... sure, frown for a moment, then don that smile and focus on the positive. Start by creating a 30-day Gratitude Journal. Every day, for 30 days, list the good things in life for which you're grateful. Your perspective is guaranteed to improve if you incorporate this simple tool into your life! Remember, a good attitude won't guarantee victory, but a bad one will absolutely guarantee defeat. *What's keeping you from starting a journal and taking this suggestion seriously?*

## reflections and intentions

my thoughts and feelings on today's FLASHPOINTS include:

my intentions and action items today include:

today I am grateful for:

# Cheering helps!
# It can be difficult to continue pushing
# once you've hit the big time.

Yes, even high achievers sometimes struggle through down cycles. If we don't recast our vision after a few wins, it's tempting to just relax and coast for a while. But, beware! It's been said, "There's just one way to coast ... and that's downhill." We're all challenged with the occasional season of low motivation. If you're in that season now, the input and inspiration of a coach or mentor could be just what you need to get back on the winning track. No high achiever reaches greatness without one. It's like having a high-impact trainer in our life who knows our capabilities, who believes in us, cheering us on from the sidelines, pushing us from strength to strength. *Who's inspiring you to push the boundaries and reach for greatness?*

## reflections and intentions

my thoughts and feelings on today's FLASHPOINTS include:

my intentions and action items today include:

today I am grateful for:

# Make friends not enemies, and you will always have eyes in the back of your head.

~ Eric Pio

After five days of prompting and prodding new ideas and thoughts to come to mind, today we review what we've discovered. It's time to take a peek back at our journaling, to review our thoughts, feelings, and action items; and see how well we did. After all, self-awareness is the key to initiate growth and realize lasting change.

## weekly reflection

reflecting on my thoughts, feelings and experiences from this past week, the top three that impacted me the most include:

my top "ta-da's" (successes) from this past week include:

my top "oh-no's" (disappointments) from this past week include:

my top "ah-ha's" (discoveries) from this past week include:

> ## A goal should scare you a little, and excite you a lot.
> ### ~ Dr. Joe Vitale

The end of the week is the best time to plan for the coming week. And at this point, you've reviewed the previous week and can be prepared to make changes and take actions based on thought, not re-action. You want to keep your goals in mind always. So today is your opportunity to look at yesterday's Weekly Reflection and decide what you're going to do and when. It is most often small tweaks that will lead to great success, fueled by a positive and grateful attitude.

## weekly intentions

my top "go get-'em's" (fixes) to implement this coming week include:

incomplete action items, that support my goals, to carry over into this coming week include: (schedule them now and be specific.)

new action items, that support my goals, for this coming week include: (schedule them now and be specific.)

something new I'm grateful for this week, and with whom I will share it:

## The high achiever is the average achiever, focused.

Considering our daily juggling act (career, family, socializing, sports, club participation, education, spiritual endeavors, health matters, etc.), it's no surprise that focusing on the simplest task can sometimes prove painful. For high achievers, the mission becomes even more taxing as we strive to serve others before serving ourselves. But, let's not confuse activity with achievement. Slow down! Taking a periodic time out is the most effective way to rejuvenate and find focus. It might be a day of digital detox away from our gadgets or the occasional 5-minute mental health break to take deep breaths and remind ourselves that we must do less to achieve more. Here's our challenge: strive for simplicity and intentionality in life and business. *What's on your plate that you can defer, delegate or delete?*

## reflections and intentions

my thoughts and feelings on today's FLASHPOINTS include:

my intentions and action items today include:

today I am grateful for:

# You're not just leading a team; you're growing a community.

We're delusional if we think we can simply gather a group of high achievers, and expect them to perform as a team with enduring growth and success. High-performing teams share a common vision, and healthy communities share common values. So, how do we set our vision-focused teams up to become a community sharing its values? Communities share deeper ties beyond the common cause of attaining a goal. Focus on the sustainability of our efforts, invest in professional and personal development of team members, empower them to become leaders, and share in the decision-making process. Think of the role of our organization as being an incubator for leaders who, in turn, recruit their own teams and grow the community with us. *How can you create a deeper community among your team?*

## reflections and intentions

my thoughts and feelings on today's FLASHPOINTS include:

my intentions and action items today include:

today I am grateful for:

# Hope for the best, plan for the worst ... and prepare contingency plans.

In *every* endeavor, it's important to consider both ends of the outcome spectrum. To experience greater significance and achievement, bold leaps are often necessary, which could lead to mistakes and failure; so having a contingency plan is simply prudent. Courageously taking on the challenge of facing "the worst" possible scenario actually gives us mental and emotional freedom to hope for, enjoy, and *pursue the best*. It's especially important as we scale our lives: a larger vision, larger home, larger clients, larger teams, etc. As uncomfortable as it might be, we must play those mental movies of worst-case scenarios so we can plan for alternate outcomes, should the ugliness actually materialize. *What worst case scenario have you been avoiding? What good can come from your worst case scenario?*

## reflections and intentions

my thoughts and feelings on today's FLASHPOINTS include:

my intentions and action items today include:

today I am grateful for:

## Service is at the core of every leadership role.

It's often through others that we realize who we really are in life. Great leaders realize that they must be of service to others; that they must encourage others to achieve greatness. Have you ever noticed yourself offering kindness and compliments to others that you often withhold from yourself? Isn't it interesting that we often place the happiness of others ahead of ourselves, even in everyday situations? Although it's a fine line between service and codependence, that's what leadership is all about—it's the perfect example of being of service to others. It's humbling to know that our courage, commitment, generosity, and passion can cause lasting improvements in the lives of others. *How will you show courage, generosity, or passion to someone today?*

## reflections and intentions

my thoughts and feelings on today's FLASHPOINTS include:

my intentions and action items today include:

today I am grateful for:

## Mediocrity only breeds more mediocrity.

The world is chock full of people satisfied with working week after week without passion, living a life of gray mediocrity—all for the grand payoff of two days a week of relaxation and two weeks a year of fun. We were created for more! As we travel our life paths toward a vision of greater things, we must remain diligent. We must strive for excellence, and we must persevere. If we don't, we're in danger of falling into the company of fools, naysayers, and energy vampires who let obstacles and fear paralyze them. One day, they'll get bitten by the hungry dog of regret. Now's the time to identify our passions and articulate our vision for greatness. *What will you do to move your vision from fantasy to reality?*

## reflections and intentions

my thoughts and feelings on today's FLASHPOINTS include:

my intentions and action items today include:

today I am grateful for:

FLASHPOINTS for achievers

> ## If everybody thought before they spoke, the silence would be deafening.
>
> ~ George Barzan

After five days of prompting and prodding new ideas and thoughts to come to mind, today we review what we've discovered. It's time to take a peek back at our journaling, to review our thoughts, feelings, and action items; and see how well we did. After all, self-awareness is the key to initiate growth and realize lasting change.

## weekly reflection

reflecting on my thoughts, feelings and experiences from this past week, the top three that impacted me the most include:


my top "ta-da's" (successes) from this past week include:


my top "oh-no's" (disappointments) from this past week include:


my top "ah-ha's" (discoveries) from this past week include:

> # When I thought I couldn't go on, I forced myself to keep going. My success is based on persistence, not luck.
>
> ## ~ Estee Lauder

The end of the week is the best time to plan for the coming week. And at this point, you've reviewed the previous week and can be prepared to make changes and take actions based on thought, not re-action. You want to keep your goals in mind always. So today is your opportunity to look at yesterday's Weekly Reflection and decide what you're going to do and when. It is most often small tweaks that will lead to great success, fueled by a positive and grateful attitude.

## weekly intentions

my top "go get-'em's" (fixes) to implement this coming week include:

incomplete action items, that support my goals, to carry over into this coming week include: (schedule them now and be specific.)

new action items, that support my goals, for this coming week include: (schedule them now and be specific.)

something new I'm grateful for this week, and with whom I will share it:

## It might not be their fault.

With good reason, we want to surround ourselves with family, friends and team members who are trustworthy, loyal, confident, and passionate. But if we want those characteristics *in abundance* around us, we need to display them *in abundance* ourselves. Translation: *we need to earn it.* Take commitment, for example. At what level are we demonstrating commitment on that high-priority project or to our team members? Are they rewarded and shown appreciation for their herculean efforts? Do we go the extra mile independent of the actions of others? As high achievers, we must first show the qualities desired in others, and then they will follow. Anything less leads to mediocrity in them and us. *Pick one of the above qualities. How well are your recent actions communicating that quality?*

## reflections and intentions

my thoughts and feelings on today's FLASHPOINTS include:

my intentions and action items today include:

today I am grateful for:

# If your dreams don't scare you, they're not big enough.

As we seek to achieve our most significant goals in life, we'll be faced with sizable challenges, which will likely draw attention to our weaknesses. Quite often those weaknesses turn into fears that can be debilitating when it comes to taking the necessary actions to overcome those challenges. We may not even be aware that we're procrastinating or having trouble taking action, because ... we're *scared*. The first step in overcoming our challenges is to become aware of the root cause of our fear. A mentor or coach can help us do that, while providing the support we need to take the second and third steps: embracing it and then moving past it. *What are you afraid of? So, now what?*

## reflections and intentions

my thoughts and feelings on today's FLASHPOINTS include:

my intentions and action items today include:

today I am grateful for:

## "You can't handle the truth!"
## ...or can you?

In the traditional workplace, staff members receive feedback from managers in the form of periodic performance reviews. Good managers also ask their employees to give them feedback as well. But is this two-way feedback enough for high achievers? No! Because our goal is to build cohesive, elite teams around us, the 360-degree review (where each person's peers, managers, and staff give feedback) is needed. *And it starts with us.* Just be clear that the purpose is for growth and improvement, not ridicule. The key to successful 360-degree reviews is our commitment to courageously accept the feedback that's offered, and make improvements where needed. What if we implemented the 360-degree review in our personal lives, too? *What will it take for you to implement your 360-degree review process?*

## reflections and intentions

my thoughts and feelings on today's FLASHPOINTS include:

my intentions and action items today include:

today I am grateful for:

## "You've got mail!" Maybe

Sorting and reading through our email takes a considerable part of each day. Often, the more active the inbox, the more clients and business opportunities. What happens when "great" emails slow down and our inbox becomes filled with ezines and newsletters? Don't confuse our communications with legitimate clients and business opportunities with an inbox full of junk! There's only one way to get back on top and be inundated with work that matters: be proactive. Hitting the refresh button will never enhance, nor create, relationships as effectively as a targeted "dialing for dollars" or "pressing the flesh" campaign. Get out there, increase your sphere of influence with those you know, and expand your horizons by meeting new people. *Does your inbox reflect your business, life, and aspirations?*

## reflections and intentions

my thoughts and feelings on today's FLASHPOINTS include:

my intentions and action items today include:

today I am grateful for:

## Do you really pick the team, or does the team pick you?

It's a delicate balance between being of service to those we lead, and them being of service to our goals and expectations. The question becomes: *Who really keeps our team going?* We're often a pillar, and seen by most as THE key component to our highly functioning team. But without the team *members*, we don't have anyone to *lead*...and a one-legged stool will quickly tip over. So, while it may seem that we're the one holding it all together, remember that without the respect and participation of our team, we won't go far. And when they pick us, not because of money or security, but because they BELIEVE in us, life can be oh, so sweet. *How can you ensure your team will pick you over and over again?*

### reflections and intentions

my thoughts and feelings on today's FLASHPOINTS include:

my intentions and action items today include:

today I am grateful for:

*I always view problems as opportunities in work clothes.*

~ Henry Kaiser

After five days of prompting and prodding new ideas and thoughts to come to mind, today we review what we've discovered. It's time to take a peek back at our journaling, to review our thoughts, feelings, and action items; and see how well we did. After all, self-awareness is the key to initiate growth and realize lasting change.

## weekly reflection

reflecting on my thoughts, feelings and experiences from this past week, the top three that impacted me the most include:

my top "ta-da's" (successes) from this past week include:

my top "oh-no's" (disappointments) from this past week include:

my top "ah-ha's" (discoveries) from this past week include:

> ## *The major value in life is not what you get.*
> ## *The major value in life is what you become.*
> ### ~ Jim Rohn

The end of the week is the best time to plan for the coming week. And at this point, you've reviewed the previous week and can be prepared to make changes and take actions based on thought, not re-action. You want to keep your goals in mind always. So today is your opportunity to look at yesterday's Weekly Reflection and decide what you're going to do and when. It is most often small tweaks that will lead to great success, fueled by a positive and grateful attitude.

## weekly intentions

my top "go get-'em's" (fixes) to implement this coming week include:

incomplete action items, that support my goals, to carry over into this coming week include: (schedule them now and be specific.)

new action items, that support my goals, for this coming week include: (schedule them now and be specific.)

something new I'm grateful for this week, and with whom I will share it:

> ## Keep your fears to yourself, but share your inspiration with others.
>
> ~Robert L Stevenson

# I OBJECT!

Quoting someone and then disagreeing with them is not something done often, but there are times when it's needed. Part of being a great leader is leading by example: forging through obstacles by determined actions, thoughts, and willpower. And when we admit our fears, and continue succeeding in spite of them, that exemplifies great leadership. Because then we're teaching others to do the same and sending the message that no matter what our fears are, we won't let them control us. Instead, we will use them for the greater good. So while it's good to share our inspiration, true inspiration comes from sharing our fears and our courage to succeed through them. *What fears on your journey are you going to share that will inspire others?*

## reflections and intentions

my thoughts and feelings on today's FLASHPOINTS include:

my intentions and action items today include:

today I am grateful for:

# World changers focus less on new systems and processes and more on a clearly articulated vision.

At the most basic level, a vision statement is meant to put words to what we're out to achieve with our business or project. On a much deeper level, however, it should be used to communicate our vision to those who can help make it happen: investors, team members, clients, and even our friends. Think of it as a mantra: *JUST DO IT* (Nike). Simple, yet powerful and memorable. It comes down to this: if we can reflexively speak our vision to others without even thinking, applause is due. But if our stakeholders can do the same, we deserve a standing ovation! Ask two of your team members to recite your vision statement. Now ask a client. *Now what are you going to do as a result?*

## reflections and intentions

my thoughts and feelings on today's FLASHPOINTS include:

my intentions and action items today include:

today I am grateful for:

# Fans build our brands.

A well-known game developer in the U.S. recently raised over a million dollars in less than 24 hours for his next release. By making the initial purchase, his customers backed his business; but as the emotional bond grew, they did more than that: they backed his vision. Think about the enormous amount of trust and belief his fans have in him, to invest money without actually having a product, without knowing much about it, and before it's even in development! What's the lesson? When we exceed expectations and make emotional connections with people, they move from being a customer, to becoming a fan. That's when we know our character is developed to a high level: people really trust us. *How are you moving from developing customers to creating fans?*

## reflections and intentions

my thoughts and feelings on today's FLASHPOINTS include:

my intentions and action items today include:

today I am grateful for:

# Counsel woven from experience, reality and love is wisdom.

Giving up on our goals is not a decision to be taken lightly. Too often, when we're frustrated, we stop believing we can make it across the finish line, and we shift attention to the next bright, shiny object. To avoid that knee-jerk, emotional response, we must seek the wisdom of our mentors and coaches to bring calm, clarity and awakening. Mentors can relate to our feelings and frustrations, and they help us work toward a sound decision that is ultimately in our best interest. Don't give up; rather, *look* up ... to *them*. Build the discipline to look up to them in both easy and hard times. Avoid isolation, as the lone-wolf journey is a treacherous one. *What plans are you making to connect with your mentor or coach?*

## reflections and intentions

my thoughts and feelings on today's FLASHPOINTS include:

my intentions and action items today include:

today I am grateful for:

# "TGIF" just took on a whole new meaning.

For most of us, we look forward to Fridays as the end of a work week, with fewer meetings, deadlines and commitments. While others are slowing down and cutting out early, Fridays can be the most productive day of the week for high achievers. It's our choice to take advantage of a bonus day full of opportunities, and resist temptation to "party" early. Granted, sometimes it's great to leave early for a weekend away—*but not every Friday!* So, how do we overcome that temptation? (1) Remind ourselves of the limited time we have to achieve the vision of reaching our fullest potential, (2) write down one thing to inch us toward achieving it, and (3) GO DO IT! *What can you do to make Friday your Opportunity Day?*

## reflections and intentions

my thoughts and feelings on today's FLASHPOINTS include:

my intentions and action items today include:

today I am grateful for:

## Who begins too much accomplishes little.

~ German Proverb

The end of the week is the best time to plan for the coming week. And at this point, you've reviewed the previous week and can be prepared to make changes and take actions based on thought, not re-action. You want to keep your goals in mind always. So today is your opportunity to look at yesterday's Weekly Reflection and decide what you're going to do and when. It is most often small tweaks that will lead to great success, fueled by a positive and grateful attitude.

### weekly reflection

reflecting on my thoughts, feelings and experiences from this past week, the top three that impacted me the most include:

my top "ta-da's" (successes) from this past week include:

my top "oh-no's" (disappointments) from this past week include:

my top "ah-ha's" (discoveries) from this past week include:

> # *Unnecessary fear of a bad decision is a major stumbling block to good decisions.*
>
> ### ~ Jim Camp

After five days of prompting and prodding new ideas and thoughts to come to mind, today we review what we've discovered. It's time to take a peek back at our journaling, to review our thoughts, feelings, and action items; and see how well we did. After all, self-awareness is the key to initiate growth and realize lasting change.

## weekly intentions

my top "go get-'em's" (fixes) to implement this coming week include:

incomplete action items, that support my goals, to carry over into this coming week include: (schedule them now and be specific.)

new action items, that support my goals, for this coming week include: (schedule them now and be specific.)

something new I'm grateful for this week, and with whom I will share it:

# If we don't attack our "to-do" list, it will attack us.

Achievers always seem to have a lengthy to-do list. We often get overwhelmed, thinking the list never ends and there just isn't enough time in the day. We let our to-do list control us, which, in reality, means others are controlling us. So, STOP THAT! Instead, let's take back control by (1) recommitting our efforts to accomplish our goals and vision, (2) marking which items are high priority as related to our goals, and (3) deleting, delegating or deferring all those that don't need our personalized attention. By doing this, we'll create breathing room, which will lead to reduced stress and increased productivity. Isn't that what we should be focusing on, anyway? *What adjustments need to be made to your to-do list to keep you from being overwhelmed?*

## reflections and intentions

my thoughts and feelings on today's FLASHPOINTS include:

my intentions and action items today include:

today I am grateful for:

# When it comes to building relationships, being interes*ted* trumps being interest*ing*.

As leaders, sometimes our role is to entertain others, and to keep them enthused and aligned with our cause. We may need to keep the fun flowing, the pace fast, and the organization moving forward to attract high performers. It's not about us being the center of attention, though. Taking time to show interest in our allies more than trying to impress them pays enormous dividends. We must get to know our team members—their hopes, dreams, and fears—and really understand what it is that inspired them to get involved with us. This not only gives us new insights into our team, but there's no better way to remind them why they joined in the first place. *How can you show you're truly interested in those working around you?*

## reflections and intentions

my thoughts and feelings on today's FLASHPOINTS include:

my intentions and action items today include:

today I am grateful for:

> ## A sense of humor is part of the art of leadership, of getting along with people, of getting things done.
>
> ~ Dwight D. Eisenhower

Sure, we want to be high achievers, but that doesn't mean we must be serious and dour in every pursuit. For the sake of sanity (of you and your team), lighten up and enjoy the journey. Too often, we get so focused on addressing the urgently important issues that face us that we forget the value of fun and laughter to our health and well-being. It's obvious that when participants of a project, team or task are happy (including ourselves)—we're more engaged and willing to put forth extra effort. Laughter is, after all, the best medicine ... so encourage smiles and laughter in those around you by introducing an element of fun every day! *What can you do to insert a more light-hearted and fun spirit into your journey?*

## reflections and intentions

my thoughts and feelings on today's FLASHPOINTS include:

my intentions and action items today include:

today I am grateful for:

## No vision, no change.
## No change, no struggle.
## No struggle, no progress.

Write down your vision statement *now*. Does it still inspire and give meaning to your life and endeavors? Does it produce the same for your team? (Are they even able to articulate it?) If not, it may need a rewrite or refresher. After years of chasing our dreams, and fighting the good fight, we sometimes realize the grip it once had on our heart (yes, our *heart*, not our head) has slipped away. We may even be heading in a different direction. If you're looking to shake things up a bit, but you're not sure where to start, ask yourself: *1. What impact am I looking to make on the world? 2. Is that where my business/life/project is headed? 3. What needs to change to align the answers?*

### reflections and intentions

my thoughts and feelings on today's FLASHPOINTS include:

my intentions and action items today include:

today I am grateful for:

## It is more blessed to give than to receive.

~ Jesus

We've been taught to give because we'll be better off for it in the long run. But that seems to go against what's becoming an increasingly common mindset: instant gratification. Sure, we'll give if we get a quick return. But even the old phrase, "What goes around comes around," which we'd all agree is true, doesn't have an associated time frame. We're much better off by giving without requiring immediate returns. While doing good with an agenda is okay, doing good without an agenda is *powerful*. Powerful for us and the world. Plus, it's an indication of our true character, which will always, eventually, be shown. *Are you giving more because you'll get more, or simply because you want to give? Write down 3 examples that prove your conclusion either way.*

## reflections and intentions

my thoughts and feelings on today's FLASHPOINTS include:

my intentions and action items today include:

today I am grateful for:

> *What you get by achieving your goals is not as important as what you become by achieving your goals.*
>
> ~ Zig Ziglar

After five days of prompting and prodding new ideas and thoughts to come to mind, today we review what we've discovered. It's time to take a peek back at our journaling, to review our thoughts, feelings, and action items; and see how well we did. After all, self-awareness is the key to initiate growth and realize lasting change.

## weekly reflection

reflecting on my thoughts, feelings and experiences from this past week, the top three that impacted me the most include:

my top "ta-da's" (successes) from this past week include:

my top "oh-no's" (disappointments) from this past week include:

my top "ah-ha's" (discoveries) from this past week include:

> # A man's word is the only thing he can give, but yet keep.
>
> ### ~ Anonymous

The end of the week is the best time to plan for the coming week. And at this point, you've reviewed the previous week and can be prepared to make changes and take actions based on thought, not re-action. You want to keep your goals in mind always. So today is your opportunity to look at yesterday's Weekly Reflection and decide what you're going to do and when. It is most often small tweaks that will lead to great success, fueled by a positive and grateful attitude.

## weekly intentions

my top "go get-'em's" (fixes) to implement this coming week include:

incomplete action items, that support my goals, to carry over into this coming week include: (schedule them now and be specific.)

new action items, that support my goals, for this coming week include: (schedule them now and be specific.)

something new I'm grateful for this week, and with whom I will share it:

# Great mentors offer fewer teachings and more awakenings.

That line of thinking that the best mentors come only from the ranks of the uber-successful needs to be reconsidered. If not, here's what can happen: (1) the mentor is so advanced that relating to them is not possible, or their methods don't work anymore; or (2) we're too intimidated to even ask that person for mentoring! A better approach is to seek someone who is simply a few steps ahead, has a heart aligned with ours, *and* to whom we can provide some value. Because life and business are about doing what we can *today* to further ourselves, and we need to be crystal clear on what that is. *How far out in front of you are your mentors? Are their values aligned with yours?*

## reflections and intentions

my thoughts and feelings on today's FLASHPOINTS include:

my intentions and action items today include:

today I am grateful for:

## Opportunities are disguised as problems. From paper boys to CEOs, what's one skill needed to take advantage of those opportunities? Problem solving!

Opportunities are problems waiting to be solved; those that solve them reap the rewards. Being a problem solver is not just for ourselves—those around us MUST be adept at it. But can we promote more effective problem solving? Consider it two sides of a coin. Each individual must: (1) possess the desire to problem solve and think creatively and (2) be comfortable with and capable of problem solving together with others. So why not emulate a sports team and practice? Do a fun problem-solving challenge at the next team meeting. It will provide insights into how each person thinks and raise the collective skill level of the team. *How well do you problem solve as a team, and what can you do to increase that?*

### reflections and intentions

my thoughts and feelings on today's FLASHPOINTS include:

my intentions and action items today include:

today I am grateful for:

## We plan for days and days and, when the time comes, we proceed to improvise.

### ~ Quicksilver, Amazing X-Men

We've all heard the adage, "If you fail to plan, you plan to fail." That's true, but only to a point. While planning gives us a roadmap to follow, it requires *action* to move down that road toward success. Unfortunately, the *real road* we're traveling down has unanticipated potholes, curves, and roadblocks which come in the form of last-minute changes and unintended obstacles. Invariably, we'll only know about them when we're about to hit them head on. Nothing is ever certain; and nothing is so important that *planning out* a course of action is more important than *getting it done.* In the cycle of Plan-Do-Review, don't forget about DO! *What projects or tasks could get you closer to your goal if you did less planning and more doing?*

## reflections and intentions

my thoughts and feelings on today's FLASHPOINTS include:

my intentions and action items today include:

today I am grateful for:

## If we're relying on our own ideas to strengthen our teams, we're very likely missing something.

Among the responsibilities of effective leaders is to create highly functioning teams and to *continually* strengthen them for battle. Sometimes new tools must be purchased, or team members subtracted or added to the mix, or opportunities provided to learn new skills. How do we determine the critical needs of our team? *Ask!* An open and honest work environment where information flows freely from top to bottom, and even sideways, is vital to the health of strong, vibrant teams. So, put your pride on the shelf, and ask them what they need. Sure, some may mention fewer working hours and increased bonuses; however, if the right team is in place, they'll be thoughtful and communicate their needs because they want to excel. *What steps will you take to strengthen your team?*

## reflections and intentions

my thoughts and feelings on today's FLASHPOINTS include:

my intentions and action items today include:

today I am grateful for:

> ## The best way to find yourself is to lose yourself in the service of others.
>
> ~ Gandhi

How do we define servant leadership? Its distinction is clear: we put the needs of others first and do what's necessary for *the team* to reach their fullest potential, rather than accumulating power and prestige for our own glory. When we become involved in the lives of our team members and discover what makes them tick, we're in a position to positively influence their behaviors and actions. Challenging ourselves and our teammates toward greater accomplishments and self improvement inspires a surge of personal and professional growth. (That's a good thing … and leads to powerful change.) Servant leadership requires a humble spirit, a caring heart and the ability to share the spotlight of success. *How well are you serving the needs of others?*

## reflections and intentions

my thoughts and feelings on today's FLASHPOINTS include:

my intentions and action items today include:

today I am grateful for:

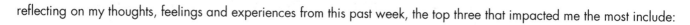

> # *The right to do something does not mean that doing it is right.*
> ### ~ William Safire

After five days of prompting and prodding new ideas and thoughts to come to mind, today we review what we've discovered. It's time to take a peek back at our journaling, to review our thoughts, feelings, and action items; and see how well we did. After all, self-awareness is the key to initiate growth and realize lasting change.

## weekly reflection

reflecting on my thoughts, feelings and experiences from this past week, the top three that impacted me the most include:

my top "ta-da's" (successes) from this past week include:

my top "oh-no's" (disappointments) from this past week include:

my top "ah-ha's" (discoveries) from this past week include:

> ## You can't have a better tomorrow if you're thinking about yesterday.
> ~ Charles Kettering

The end of the week is the best time to plan for the coming week. And at this point, you've reviewed the previous week and can be prepared to make changes and take actions based on thought, not re-action. You want to keep your goals in mind always. So today is your opportunity to look at yesterday's Weekly Reflection and decide what you're going to do and when. It is most often small tweaks that will lead to great success, fueled by a positive and grateful attitude.

## weekly intentions

my top "go get-'em's" (fixes) to implement this coming week include:

incomplete action items, that support my goals, to carry over into this coming week include: (schedule them now and be specific.)

new action items, that support my goals, for this coming week include: (schedule them now and be specific.)

something new I'm grateful for this week, and with whom I will share it:

## What do we call someone who has given up on their dreams? Even if they are only 18, we call them OLD!

As kids, we had plenty of hopes, aspirations and dreams. We wanted to be an astronaut, rock star, princess, fireman, etc. Now that we're older, we've gotten more "realistic." But should we be? (Realistic, that is?) Just search the web for "older entrepreneurs" and read their stories. These people have kept their hopes and dreams of success not just alive but *vibrant*, and they're cultivating lives of significance. In their minds, they *minimized their limitations* and simply believed it could happen—NOTHING stands in their way. The fact is, there's really no barrier any of us can't overcome to make our dreams come true. *Have you lost sight of your big vision? What needs to happen to prevent you from the dreaded words, "I'll do that ... some day"?*

## reflections and intentions

my thoughts and feelings on today's FLASHPOINTS include:

my intentions and action items today include:

today I am grateful for:

# Sometimes what's on our mind is like old milk ...if not dealt with, it can start to stink.

Ever had a thought on your mind so big that it caused you major distractions in just about every area of life? When it's standing in our way and keeping us from being fully present with our business or project, we have two options: One, we can ignore it and continue with the reduced productivity, lack of focus, and inability to deeply connect with people; or two, the more difficult but most effective option, DEAL WITH IT! When it comes time, we must be brazen and address it head on—within ourselves or with the assistance of others. It's time to remove the nonproductive mental and emotional chatter and create room again for what's really important—positive, uplifting mental messages. *What negative mental chatter do you have that needs to be removed?*

## reflections and intentions

my thoughts and feelings on today's FLASHPOINTS include:

my intentions and action items today include:

today I am grateful for:

> In all we do and don't do,
> In all we say and don't say,
> We are all teachers ... or should be.

The following quote is from an unexpected source, yet it's full of wisdom. On an episode of the television show *Glee,* one student says to another's father, "Help your son honor his gift." Like that father, we need to consider the important role we play in the lives of those around us—helping them to achieve their goals, moving them closer to their fullest potential, or helping them avoid crucial mistakes. We need not overcomplicate relationships ... they're simply about being available, listening, asking probing questions, offering encouragement and an offering an occasional nudge toward a more focused sight picture. Simply put: serve *others.* This amounts to a significant contribution to *their* life! *How are you being a mentor or coach in someone else's life?*

## reflections and intentions

my thoughts and feelings on today's FLASHPOINTS include:

my intentions and action items today include:

today I am grateful for:

# "Peak" a-boo, I see you!

While there are guidelines for how to work at our peak, we're all unique creations, so there are no hard and fast rules. As leaders, we need to show others the way to peak performance, but it starts with understanding our own habits and needs. Ask these questions: Is slow and steady best, or is an impending deadline better? Are you energized being around others in your industry, or is it better to work with just a few close colleagues? Does travel suit you well, or do you prefer to stay home? Whatever the answers, we must be aggressive in factoring them into our schedules and our environments—the world needs us at our best as often as possible. *What are the things that help you perform at your peak?*

## reflections and intentions

my thoughts and feelings on today's FLASHPOINTS include:

my intentions and action items today include:

today I am grateful for:

> # The best businesses create a flexible environment that addresses the needs of their team. If the team needs are met, business needs are met.

What type of work environment have we created for our team? Is it stuck in the industrial age, serving the needs of the system, or is it serving the needs of the people? Yes, *flexibility* in the areas of working hours, leave arrangements, and working from home are crucial to improving team member engagement … but true flexibility is when people are given a chance to do something special, to take on a new challenge, to achieve mastery in some new area of interest. As the economy shifts and change occurs faster than ever, our teams must keep pace. But it's only a loyal, energetic, and fully engaged workforce that makes those transformations quickly. *So what do you need to do to create that type of environment for your team?*

## reflections and intentions

my thoughts and feelings on today's FLASHPOINTS include:

my intentions and action items today include:

today I am grateful for:

> **Serving others should be an honor and a privilege, not a 'duty'.**
> ~ Theodore Mouser

After five days of prompting and prodding new ideas and thoughts to come to mind, today we review what we've discovered. It's time to take a peek back at our journaling, to review our thoughts, feelings, and action items; and see how well we did. After all, self-awareness is the key to initiate growth and realize lasting change.

## weekly reflection

reflecting on my thoughts, feelings and experiences from this past week, the top three that impacted me the most include:

my top "ta-da's" (successes) from this past week include:

my top "oh-no's" (disappointments) from this past week include:

my top "ah-ha's" (discoveries) from this past week include:

> ## If you want to achieve a high goal, you're going to have to take some chances.
>
> ### ~ Alberto Salazar

The end of the week is the best time to plan for the coming week. And at this point, you've reviewed the previous week and can be prepared to make changes and take actions based on thought, not re-action. You want to keep your goals in mind always. So today is your opportunity to look at yesterday's Weekly Reflection and decide what you're going to do and when. It is most often small tweaks that will lead to great success, fueled by a positive and grateful attitude.

## weekly intentions

my top "go get-'em's" (fixes) to implement this coming week include:

incomplete action items, that support my goals, to carry over into this coming week include: (schedule them now and be specific.)

new action items, that support my goals, for this coming week include: (schedule them now and be specific.)

something new I'm grateful for this week, and with whom I will share it:

# Going for "it" is much more than ordering cupcakes and cappuccinos.

If only success could be as simple as placing our order from the take-out menu and waiting for it to arrive at our doorstep or be delivered through our car window. Ah, but that's wishful thinking. That kind of success is cheap and rare, only attained by lottery winners (and those winnings are often quickly lost). The rest of us have to get in the kitchen, blend the ingredients and grind the coffee beans ourselves. Translation: it takes sustained, positive action, following a proven plan, and heading in the right direction to realize enduring success. World changers, dream builders, and achievement seekers consistently take small steps every day toward their goals and fullest potential. *So what recipe are you engaged in to complete your order?*

## reflections and intentions

my thoughts and feelings on today's FLASHPOINTS include:

my intentions and action items today include:

today I am grateful for:

# There's power in the "we."

Our journey toward significance, influence, and achievement likely began with a simple vision, known only to ourselves (and perhaps a small band of believers). As we gain momentum, however, and begin to enlist supporters to our cause, we need to make the journey less about us and more about them. Enduring success requires we ensure our own agenda is aligned with the best outcome for the entire team. To increase team member engagement and inspiration, each action and every communication must come from the framework of "we", not "I." When we transform our thinking and recognize that our primary mission is about serving our teams, then trust, cohesion, and allegiance will most surely follow. And next? Success! *How often do you use "I," when you should be saying "we"?*

## reflections and intentions

my thoughts and feelings on today's FLASHPOINTS include:

my intentions and action items today include:

today I am grateful for:

# The best way to lead for a brighter tomorrow is to genuinely connect with team members today.

High achievers recognize the importance of positive imagery and visualization to obtain the loftiest of goals. We understand that, in every area of our lives, we should have a defined vision that guides our daily journey. But how often, and how effectively, have we expressed our vision to the people we've entrusted to help us? A better question is, *have they caught the vision bug?* It may seem "adequate" to thoroughly articulate the specific job duties we expect our team members to accomplish, but we really want more than that, don't we? Vision TRAINING and vision ADOPTION for every stakeholder is crucial for optimum productivity and accomplishment. *How have you ensured that your vision has become your team's vision?*

## reflections and intentions

my thoughts and feelings on today's FLASHPOINTS include:

my intentions and action items today include:

today I am grateful for:

# Consumers continue to climb the savvy ladder, and there's only one way to respond.

Everyone's a consumer *and* a marketer. As consumers, we're accustomed to questioning relationships, products and brands because we've all been bitten in the past—we've learned something we didn't like, or our expectations simply weren't met. And, as marketers, we're even more vulnerable; from global competition to shrinking consumer budgets, to the white noise from social media channels, we're left with only one way to respond: *tell it like it is!* We're all a little suspicious of glitz, glam, and flowery slogans, but we find power in truth-telling and sharing exactly what consumers need to know to make the best decision *for them*. With time, we'll start developing fans; and when that happens, they'll tell others. *How can you be more authentic with your personal and professional messaging?*

## reflections and intentions

my thoughts and feelings on today's FLASHPOINTS include:

my intentions and action items today include:

today I am grateful for:

# When the student is ready, the teacher will appear. But what does it take to be ready?

Coaches and mentors reveal themselves throughout our lives—in school, the workplace, and even in our social circles. But have we always been ready to receive them? Being coachable requires taking the time to be aware of our gifts, attitudes, and limiting beliefs—and also being open to wisdom that others might impart to us. Self-awareness is key, which requires us to be humble and to give our egos a swift kick in the rear! Just like the saying, "You can lead a horse to water, but you can't make him drink," there is only so much experience and know-how these people can pour into our lives—the rest is up to us. Are you ready to receive? *What do you need to do to be more coachable?*

## reflections and intentions

my thoughts and feelings on today's FLASHPOINTS include:

my intentions and action items today include:

today I am grateful for:

> # Nurture your mind with great thoughts for you will never go any higher than you think.
>
> ~ Benjamin Disraeli

After five days of prompting and prodding new ideas and thoughts to come to mind, today we review what we've discovered. It's time to take a peek back at our journaling, to review our thoughts, feelings, and action items; and see how well we did. After all, self-awareness is the key to initiate growth and realize lasting change.

## weekly reflection

reflecting on my thoughts, feelings and experiences from this past week, the top three that impacted me the most include:

my top "ta-da's" (successes) from this past week include:

my top "oh-no's" (disappointments) from this past week include:

my top "ah-ha's" (discoveries) from this past week include:

## Dig the well before you are thirsty.
~ Chinese Proverb

The end of the week is the best time to plan for the coming week. And at this point, you've reviewed the previous week and can be prepared to make changes and take actions based on thought, not re-action. You want to keep your goals in mind always. So today is your opportunity to look at yesterday's Weekly Reflection and decide what you're going to do and when. It is most often small tweaks that will lead to great success, fueled by a positive and grateful attitude.

### weekly intentions

my top "go get-'em's" (fixes) to implement this coming week include:

incomplete action items, that support my goals, to carry over into this coming week include: (schedule them now and be specific.)

new action items, that support my goals, for this coming week include: (schedule them now and be specific.)

something new I'm grateful for this week, and with whom I will share it:

FLASHPOINTS for achievers

## Excellence begins with attitude.

Nothing is less attractive than a "professional" second-guessing themselves. It hurts morale, sales, networks, and even the attraction and retention of good teammates. Our highly competitive society craves talking to, learning from, and being in community with other high-performers, where excellence is the minimum standard for success. It's up to us to figure out how to be the best in our industry, and how to be the best possible versions of ourselves. That involves choice—the choice of striving for excellence in all we do. This doesn't mean being snooty when telling others about ourselves and our pursuit of excellence, but it does mean having confidence in ourselves, our abilities, and the path we've chosen to master. *What are you doing to increase your self-confidence and your abilities?*

### reflections and intentions

my thoughts and feelings on today's FLASHPOINTS include:

my intentions and action items today include:

today I am grateful for:

# If you are traveling with children, or are seated next to someone who needs assistance, place the mask on yourself first, then offer assistance.

We've heard the safety presentation by the flight attendants regarding the use of oxygen masks should there be a sudden drop in cabin pressure. If we're going to provide optimum, long-term value to our team, we must take care of ourselves first: physically, spiritually, mentally, and emotionally. Creating time for things like working out, regular break times, proper rest, and better planning to avoid the constant need for late night work contributes to that goal and sends a powerful message about priorities to our family and teams. Even taking time off to volunteer for a worthy cause does wonders for team morale, a sense of team cohesion and spiritual fulfillment. *How are you ensuring that both your and your team's needs are being met? Maybe you should ask them.*

## reflections and intentions

my thoughts and feelings on today's FLASHPOINTS include:

my intentions and action items today include:

today I am grateful for:

> ## One of the first rules of science is, if somebody delivers a secret weapon to you, you'd better use it.
>
> —Herbert Simon

Ah, the secret weapon. What is it? It's our *"why."* The reason *why* we're focused on our cause. The reason *why* we're committed to making a difference. And it's unique to each of us. No one else is driven by the same reasons, passions, or motivations; nor do they possess our background or upbringing. Our uniqueness is what we craft into our true and authentic story ... it's what makes us appealing to those that we're meant to serve and to be surrounded by. Our "why" spurs us on toward rapid action and helps us make decisions. But, lose touch with it, and others will lose touch with it soon after, and our journey could become crippling. *What's your "why", and how deeply are you connected to it?*

## reflections and intentions

my thoughts and feelings on today's FLASHPOINTS include:

my intentions and action items today include:

today I am grateful for:

# The teeter-totter of being a leader: one side is our tasks, the other side is our team's tasks

Why are we inundated with to-dos, yet others don't seem to have enough to keep busy? At times, we're going to feel like we're doing everything, with little help from others. Worse, we'll start making the mistake of thinking, "It's better to just do this myself." Leadership doesn't mean taking on the world by ourselves—it means being of service to our team ... and distributing the efforts and workload appropriately. On occasion, we'll be the driving force toward success; at other times, our team will take point on achieving our goals. Understanding when to ask more from teammates and when to ask more from ourselves is a sign of maturity and helps everyone realize victory. *Whose turn is it to push up your team's teeter-totter?*

## reflections and intentions

my thoughts and feelings on today's FLASHPOINTS include:

my intentions and action items today include:

today I am grateful for:

## I'll know I've made it when ...

We are so motivated to succeed in life and we drive to beat our competition. But when does it stop? When do we finally get to say, "I've achieved what I set out to do?" Probably never – as leaders and innovators, we know there is always more to be achieved in life, and we want another piece of it! We can get caught up in executing our ideas, so much so, that we don't take time to focus on what the end vision is. What if this means we are achieving our coveted success right now, but haven't acknowledged it? *Take a few moments now to envision for yourself how you will know when you've made it. What will life look and feel for you?*

### reflections and intentions

my thoughts and feelings on today's FLASHPOINTS include:

my intentions and action items today include:

today I am grateful for:

# I never exaggerate. I just remember big.

~ Chi Chi Rodriguez

After five days of prompting and prodding new ideas and thoughts to come to mind, today we review what we've discovered. It's time to take a peek back at our journaling, to review our thoughts, feelings, and action items; and see how well we did. After all, self-awareness is the key to initiate growth and realize lasting change.

## weekly reflection

reflecting on my thoughts, feelings and experiences from this past week, the top three that impacted me the most include:

my top "ta-da's" (successes) from this past week include:

my top "oh-no's" (disappointments) from this past week include:

my top "ah-ha's" (discoveries) from this past week include:

> ## The two most powerful warriors are patience and time.
> ### ~ Leo Tolstoy

The end of the week is the best time to plan for the coming week. And at this point, you've reviewed the previous week and can be prepared to make changes and take actions based on thought, not re-action. You want to keep your goals in mind always. So today is your opportunity to look at yesterday's Weekly Reflection and decide what you're going to do and when. It is most often small tweaks that will lead to great success, fueled by a positive and grateful attitude.

## weekly intentions

my top "go get-'em's" (fixes) to implement this coming week include:

incomplete action items, that support my goals, to carry over into this coming week include: (schedule them now and be specific.)

new action items, that support my goals, for this coming week include: (schedule them now and be specific.)

something new I'm grateful for this week, and with whom I will share it:

# The "person" part of "personal stories" connects with other persons.

The most popular public speakers are those who are transparent and share detailed, sometimes embarrassing personal stories with sincerity. It's their honesty and dedication to connect with the audience that causes us to fall in love with them. It's inspiring and helpful and creates a strong connection, making us trust them immediately. It takes guts to do this in public, so it's not for the faint of heart. It's time, however, that we summon the courage to help our team and business associates by allowing them to get to know the real us! Consider that for the people in our lives to back us 100% and play the role we need them to, they deserve the real us. *With whom do you share the real you? Is that enough?*

## reflections and intentions

my thoughts and feelings on today's FLASHPOINTS include:

my intentions and action items today include:

today I am grateful for:

## The easiest person to fool is yourself.

The Dunning-Kruger effect says we can either underestimate or overestimate our abilities, as we're simply too close to ourselves to be objective. On one hand, we don't notice our flaws; on the other hand, we downplay our skills, talents and strengths. With maturity, both perspectives can be adjusted and fine-tuned, but having a mentor is the quickest way to do that. Engaging a trusted advisor or someone in the community that we'd love to build a relationship with may be the key to illuminating those blind spots. The goal isn't to fix our blind spots, but to become aware of them so we can remember to check for them as we're driving down the road of life. *What do others see in you that you're not seeing in yourself?*

## reflections and intentions

my thoughts and feelings on today's FLASHPOINTS include:

my intentions and action items today include:

today I am grateful for:

# If a leader's "in-office" hours are greater than their "out-of-office" hours, something better change soon.

It's a no-brainer: to consistently improve, evolve and grow our business or project, we must be evangelizing our efforts and seeing our product or service in use. CONSTANTLY. And while working in a comfy-cozy office with pictures of family on the wall can be productive, it's vital to spend *intentional* time with clients and associates—time away from "the books." Examining the ratio of hours spent in versus out of the office can determine if we're thriving or on a dangerous road to failure. Plus, our creativity, energy, and love for what we do will only be strengthened when we share ourselves with others. *Look at your calendar for the past month and see what your "in" versus "out" hours are like. How can you improve on it?*

## reflections and intentions

my thoughts and feelings on today's FLASHPOINTS include:

my intentions and action items today include:

today I am grateful for:

## To really connect with your team, lose the "big boss" filter.

There's a fine line between over-sharing and authenticity; but the thickness of that line is debatable. It's challenging, as leaders, to let our guard down for fear of getting too personal with our team. But it's important for them to have some personal connection with who we *really* are, as we're on the quest for success together, and there will be times when they'll have to pick US up. Ideas for getting *real:* (1) Share a failure or embarrassing moment. (2) Tell about one of the happiest moments of your life. (3) Share the "why" of the business or project. Final hint: Loosen up! Use conversational language, since this isn't a presentation for the White House. *How can you create your missing connection or bolster an existing one?*

## reflections and intentions

my thoughts and feelings on today's FLASHPOINTS include:

my intentions and action items today include:

today I am grateful for:

# Passion doesn't take out the trash, but if the trash stays, things start to stink.

Don't be fooled: there will always be some tasks that we're NOT impassioned to complete. Although there's no skip or fast-forward button in the real world, we can speed up those uninspiring tasks that bring down our mood and morale. How? First, we'll need an attitude adjustment, recognizing that these task are necessary and will help us reach the prize. Second, we develop a plan to delete, defer or delegate those uninspiring tasks within some set period of time. Third, we look for ways to make the un-fun, fun ... or at least more interesting. Can you set a speed record doing it or liven it up by changing colors? Remember, how we approach those unwanted tasks is our choice. *How will you add fun to the un-fun?*

## reflections and intentions

my thoughts and feelings on today's FLASHPOINTS include:

my intentions and action items today include:

today I am grateful for:

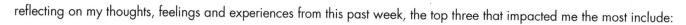

## We all need to take great interest in the future because we will spend the rest of our life there.

~ Anonymous

After five days of prompting and prodding new ideas and thoughts to come to mind, today we review what we've discovered. It's time to take a peek back at our journaling, to review our thoughts, feelings, and action items; and see how well we did. After all, self-awareness is the key to initiate growth and realize lasting change.

## weekly reflection

reflecting on my thoughts, feelings and experiences from this past week, the top three that impacted me the most include:

my top "ta-da's" (successes) from this past week include:

my top "oh-no's" (disappointments) from this past week include:

my top "ah-ha's" (discoveries) from this past week include:

> ## As we express our gratitude, we must never forget that the highest appreciation is not to utter words, but to live by them.
> ~ John F. Kennedy

The end of the week is the best time to plan for the coming week. And at this point, you've reviewed the previous week and can be prepared to make changes and take actions based on thought, not re-action. You want to keep your goals in mind always. So today is your opportunity to look at yesterday's Weekly Reflection and decide what you're going to do and when. It is most often small tweaks that will lead to great success, fueled by a positive and grateful attitude.

## weekly intentions

my top "go get-'em's" (fixes) to implement this coming week include:

incomplete action items, that support my goals, to carry over into this coming week include: (schedule them now and be specific.)

new action items, that support my goals, for this coming week include: (schedule them now and be specific.)

something new I'm grateful for this week, and with whom I will share it:

# Gain traction with a dis-traction!

Sometimes, what helps us get through a leadership crisis or crossroads is a distraction (and I don't mean excessive TV watching). Taking on a new leadership role, maybe just a minor one in a new or different community, can spur fresh ideas and provide both relief *and* clarity. While it might feel like we're adding new responsibilities to an already hectic life, which could cause us to go deeper into the sinkhole of problems, it'll likely do the opposite … especially if we're truly committed to serving others. Leading in an entirely new environment can remind us of our God-given gifts, hone our skills and increase our confidence. *Are there leadership opportunities around you that could take your mind off being a leader?*

## reflections and intentions

my thoughts and feelings on today's FLASHPOINTS include:

my intentions and action items today include:

today I am grateful for:

# When you innovate, you've got to be prepared for everyone telling you you're nuts.

~ Larry Ellison

Have you ever encountered doubt or disbelief after explaining a monster goal? If not, you're one of the lucky ones. Have you found yourself on the receiving end of a cringe, eye roll, shake of the head or the "You're kidding me, right?" look? Don't fret, it's just part of the innovation territory. We're better off being surrounded by people who are open-minded, supportive, and have faith in us. Yet we do need both types of people on our team: ones to warn us and others to bolster us. We should decide to pursue our goals based on our own gut feel, balanced with the proper perspective received from both the negative Nellies and the positive Pollies. *How will you dare to be different and trust yourself for your vision?*

## reflections and intentions

my thoughts and feelings on today's FLASHPOINTS include:

my intentions and action items today include:

today I am grateful for:

> # Failure is unimportant.
> # It takes courage to make a fool of yourself.
>
> ~ Charlie Chaplin

Don't be afraid to look foolish. Relish being the fool. History is littered with many so-called fools that time has since rebutted. Be a fool for your work, be a fool at play, be a fool for love, be a fool for family, be a fool for workmates, be a fool for customers, be a fool for life. With humor and time, it will be revealed that when a person loves their work, loves their play, loves their love, loves their family, loves their workmates, loves their customers … they love their life. *In what area do you need to be foolish, so that you can love in that area more?*

## reflections and intentions

my thoughts and feelings on today's FLASHPOINTS include:

my intentions and action items today include:

today I am grateful for:

# Behaviors really should be spelled Be-Have-Yours.

Often in life, we get an urge and, without thinking, we just go with it. That's called a trigger, and it's the beginning of a routine that leads to some type of reward. If we're not careful, these triggers start getting in the way of productivity and performance. Triggers are like the buzz or ding of the smartphone (or a time of day that leads us to grab a doughnut). We need to slow things down, become intentional with our choices, and write them down in this FLASHPOINTS daily journal. We can then change the routines that result from the urges and replace them with behavior we consciously want. *What are the things that get you side-tracked from what you want to do and should be doing?*

## reflections and intentions

my thoughts and feelings on today's FLASHPOINTS include:

my intentions and action items today include:

today I am grateful for:

## Inspiration is contagious.
## Get your team infected!

Think back to a project you've been involved with when you had the most fun, experienced the most success, or achieved the most results. Chances are, the teammates around you were experiencing a severe case of inspiration ... often passed down from a leader who was as passionate as they were motivational. Inspiration is the most powerful trade secret to getting a project off the ground; it's the glue that keeps a team working together and the force that swiftly creates a groundswell of believers to enlist in the cause. *How inspired are you today, and how will you infect the people in your life?*

## reflections and intentions

my thoughts and feelings on today's FLASHPOINTS include:

my intentions and action items today include:

today I am grateful for:

> ## Don't worry when you are not recognized, but strive to be worthy of recognition.
>
> ~ Abraham Lincoln

After five days of prompting and prodding new ideas and thoughts to come to mind, today we review what we've discovered. It's time to take a peek back at our journaling, to review our thoughts, feelings, and action items; and see how well we did. After all, self-awareness is the key to initiate growth and realize lasting change.

## weekly reflection

reflecting on my thoughts, feelings and experiences from this past week, the top three that impacted me the most include:

my top "ta-da's" (successes) from this past week include:

my top "oh-no's" (disappointments) from this past week include:

my top "ah-ha's" (discoveries) from this past week include:

> # *Great minds discuss ideas;*
> # *average minds discuss events;*
> # *small minds discuss people.*
> ### ~ Eleanor Roosevelt

The end of the week is the best time to plan for the coming week. And at this point, you've reviewed the previous week and can be prepared to make changes and take actions based on thought, not re-action. You want to keep your goals in mind always. So today is your opportunity to look at yesterday's Weekly Reflection and decide what you're going to do and when. It is most often small tweaks that will lead to great success, fueled by a positive and grateful attitude.

## weekly intentions

my top "go get-'em's" (fixes) to implement this coming week include:

incomplete action items, that support my goals, to carry over into this coming week include: (schedule them now and be specific.)

new action items, that support my goals, for this coming week include: (schedule them now and be specific.)

something new I'm grateful for this week, and with whom I will share it:

## Integrity means taking action even when it isn't asked, because it's true to who we are.

The people in our life believe us to be a certain kind of person based on the actions they observe from us when *we're* not looking. They probably have a much better impression of us than we have of ourselves. So sometimes, staying true to who we *really* are means taking actions, even when we're not aren't asked to—because it's the *right* thing to do. It's challenging to seize every personal growth opportunity that comes our way, but when people look up to us as a leader, achiever, friend, and world changer—although it's tough, don't we want to be that person for them? *What out-of-the-ordinary action will you take today to be true to who you really are?*

## reflections and intentions

my thoughts and feelings on today's FLASHPOINTS include:

my intentions and action items today include:

today I am grateful for:

## It ain't obstacles that stand in our way; it simply comes down to you and me.

Yes, the only thing standing between us and our goals is *us*, and it comes down to action. Sadly, knowing this and feeling inspired to take determined action can be miles apart. We can, however, start to bridge that gap by working a little smarter and contributing a little more to get things done. But sometimes, the extra pressure can bog us down, like we've been bitten by the paralysis bug. So, what's the antidote? Flexibility. Reflect, reassess, and ask: Does it really need to be done now? What are the odds of actually getting it done now? What will the consequence or reward be as a result? And how can planning be improved next time? *Which of your goals truly need more of you, and which just need revising?*

### reflections and intentions

my thoughts and feelings on today's FLASHPOINTS include:

my intentions and action items today include:

today I am grateful for:

# Help other causes get ahead ... even ahead of your very own.

I *hate* the classic networking events, because they're all about *taking*. Successful networking, like successful relationships, are more about adding value to another person's cause, rather than focusing on the rewards we might reap. Community (and the world, for that matter) is built on successful relationships with business partners, neighbors, team members, competitors, loved ones, and society stakeholders. When our focus is on serving the needs of those around us, we become a positive light, and people are drawn to us. One positive action for someone, other than ourselves, can open up a world of networks, turning our focus on *their* cause into value for *our* cause. *How will you contribute to a cause other than your own this week?*

## reflections and intentions

my thoughts and feelings on today's FLASHPOINTS include:

my intentions and action items today include:

today I am grateful for:

## How do you know if a dream is worth putting on the gloves, getting into the ring and getting bloodied?

Achievers have many ideas, hopes, and dreams across a lifetime. But which is worthy of our blood, sweat and tears? If we've dreamed it more than once, it must have some measure of importance. Then it might just need a little focus. First, think about the daydreams we wander to most often because, for some reason, these have a special connection to us. Next, prioritize: are any of the dreams time-sensitive, meaning should we go after them ahead of others? Third, tell a few trusted advisors to discover how much passion we have as we work through the minefield of figuring out how to sell it. Because then we'll end up selling to our number-one customer—ourselves. *What dream of yours is worth fighting for?*

### reflections and intentions

my thoughts and feelings on today's FLASHPOINTS include:

my intentions and action items today include:

today I am grateful for:

## Which is worse, talking too much or talking too little?
### BOTH!

Because we're constantly meeting new people in social settings, on the street, and in our business dealings, having a forthcoming, open communication style is helpful. We never know when we'll be able to serve others or to be served. Yet serving requires *connecting with* people in the way that *they* require the connection. We may need to initiate a conversation, so we must be prepared to talk, but we also must be an observer, questioner, listener, and learner. Taking the lead in a conversation might occasionally be necessary, but taking the back seat may be more useful. We *already* know what we know, so if we want to learn, lead and achieve, listening and probing is a must. How will you ensure that in today's conversations, you'll listen and learn?

## reflections and intentions

my thoughts and feelings on today's FLASHPOINTS include:

my intentions and action items today include:

today I am grateful for:

> ## We must take change by the hand or rest assuredly, change will take us by the throat.
> ~ Winston Churchill

After five days of prompting and prodding new ideas and thoughts to come to mind, today we review what we've discovered. It's time to take a peek back at our journaling, to review our thoughts, feelings, and action items; and see how well we did. After all, self-awareness is the key to initiate growth and realize lasting change.

## weekly reflection

reflecting on my thoughts, feelings and experiences from this past week, the top three that impacted me the most include:

my top "ta-da's" (successes) from this past week include:

my top "oh-no's" (disappointments) from this past week include:

my top "ah-ha's" (discoveries) from this past week include:

> ## The pain we feel when someone leaves our life is in direct proportion to the joy they bring while a part of our life...
>
> ~ Javan

The end of the week is the best time to plan for the coming week. And at this point, you've reviewed the previous week and can be prepared to make changes and take actions based on thought, not re-action. You want to keep your goals in mind always. So today is your opportunity to look at yesterday's Weekly Reflection and decide what you're going to do and when. It is most often small tweaks that will lead to great success, fueled by a positive and grateful attitude.

## weekly intentions

my top "go get-'em's" (fixes) to implement this coming week include:

incomplete action items, that support my goals, to carry over into this coming week include: (schedule them now and be specific.)

new action items, that support my goals, for this coming week include: (schedule them now and be specific.)

something new I'm grateful for this week, and with whom I will share it:

> ## Service is at the core of every leadership role. Great leaders acknowledges that they must be of service to others in order to achieve greatness.

It is often through others that we realize who we really are in life. For example, have you ever noticed that we offer kindness and compliments to others, yet we don't reward ourselves with the same? Interesting isn't it, that we often place the happiness of others ahead of ourselves, even in everyday-life situations? But that's what leadership is all about—it's the perfect example of service to others. Courage, encouragement, generosity, and passion can create lasting improvements in the lives of those around us ... resulting in a more vibrant, trusting, cohesive community. *How can you better serve your team and community in the next week?*

## reflections and intentions

my thoughts and feelings on today's FLASHPOINTS include:

my intentions and action items today include:

today I am grateful for:

# Forgiveness starts with the most important person: YOURSELF.

Having an exceptional life comes with a boatload of decision-making and risk-taking. Sometimes outcomes don't match expectations, which leads to that dreaded F-word: FAILURE. And as people who take responsibility for our own actions, we're often quick to point the finger and lay blame on the same person over and over: ourselves. Dwelling on these negative experiences doesn't make them any less so—in fact, quite the opposite. Yet ignoring failures is also a mistake—we must embrace them, learn, and move on. Most importantly, we must forgive ourselves and let go of the negativity. So, next time the mental blame-game starts, we shouldn't be too hard on ourselves; we're all only human, after all. *How can you embrace your humanity and cut yourself a break?*

## reflections and intentions

my thoughts and feelings on today's FLASHPOINTS include:

my intentions and action items today include:

today I am grateful for:

## It takes a great leader to congratulate others for the success they have pioneered.

You've heard it said many times before: "Nothing great was ever accomplished alone." Great leaders recognize this fact and attribute their success to their teams. Think about that for a minute—every achievement in your life, every success, has been a result of the actions of many, not just your own. Sure, it takes a great leader to lead a successful team, but it also takes a great team to support that leader and to take on their goals as their very own. *How do you reward those who have achieved success with you?*

## reflections and intentions

my thoughts and feelings on today's FLASHPOINTS include:

my intentions and action items today include:

today I am grateful for:

# Leave your mistakes where you made them.

Made a mistake lately? Sure, everybody has, right? Of course. Now, are we going to learn from it and move on or carry it around, weighing us down? Let's think of ourselves as a budget airliner ready to take off on a journey toward success. We have a certain weight limit, so we can only take the essentials. Let's not weigh our journey down by worrying about our mistakes of the past. Let's learn what we can and leave those mistakes where we made them. The bird in the sky does not mourn the worm it missed, but anticipates the worm to come. *How can you apply lessons from a recent mistake to improve your situation this week?*

## reflections and intentions

my thoughts and feelings on today's FLASHPOINTS include:

my intentions and action items today include:

today I am grateful for:

## The ultimate condemnation is indifference. What do people say about you behind your back?

What sounds like a fairly contentious question, is not meant to be. When we think of leaders and entrepreneurs, there are certain characteristics that usually come to mind: open-minded, innovative, visionary, amicable, assertive, inspirational and honorable. When people are describing you when you're out of the room (don't be shocked, this does happen!), what words do you think they're using? Would the description of the real you, based on what they see in everyday interactions, come close to the leader you aspire to be? Communication (both verbal and non-verbal) is an interesting thing ... actions, after all, speak louder than words, right? *What are the five characteristics you want people to recognize in you?*

### reflections and intentions

my thoughts and feelings on today's FLASHPOINTS include:

my intentions and action items today include:

today I am grateful for:

> ## All of my growth is based NOT on what I know, but on what I learn.
> ### ~ John Maxwell

After five days of prompting and prodding new ideas and thoughts to come to mind, today we review what we've discovered. It's time to take a peek back at our journaling, to review our thoughts, feelings, and action items; and see how well we did. After all, self-awareness is the key to initiate growth and realize lasting change.

## weekly reflection

reflecting on my thoughts, feelings and experiences from this past week, the top three that impacted me the most include:

my top "ta-da's" (successes) from this past week include:

my top "oh-no's" (disappointments) from this past week include:

my top "ah-ha's" (discoveries) from this past week include:

> # The mind is like a parachute.
> # It doesn't work until it's open.
> ## ~ Sam Johnson

The end of the week is the best time to plan for the coming week. And at this point, you've reviewed the previous week and can be prepared to make changes and take actions based on thought, not re-action. You want to keep your goals in mind always. So today is your opportunity to look at yesterday's Weekly Reflection and decide what you're going to do and when. It is most often small tweaks that will lead to great success, fueled by a positive and grateful attitude.

## weekly intentions

my top "go get-'em's" (fixes) to implement this coming week include:

incomplete action items, that support my goals, to carry over into this coming week include: (schedule them now and be specific.)

new action items, that support my goals, for this coming week include: (schedule them now and be specific.)

something new I'm grateful for this week, and with whom I will share it:

> # We've already succeeded often enough to know only we can stop ourselves.

Pursuing what we want with dedication and envisioning our eventual success is likely already a strong part of us. Being in business and succeeding is really not all that different from being a successful employee, parent or student. The next time we're tempted to put a lid on our dreams because they seem too audacious or mind-blowing, know that we've already accomplished many things that other people haven't. Yes, there are uncertainties all around us, but they were there in the past and will be there in the future—but haven't we already succeeded in spite of them? It really comes down to two questions: *Despite the barriers, is my dream or goal important enough that I'll give it a shot? And why?*

## reflections and intentions

my thoughts and feelings on today's FLASHPOINTS include:

my intentions and action items today include:

today I am grateful for:

## Describe yourself in three words ... go!

It's a common question when you're writing your bio, interviewing, or entering a competition—but no matter how many times the question is asked, the answer never seems to come any easier. It's just three words, but for some reason, it's difficult to commit to writing them down. When listing your three words, you'll likely realize a couple of things: (1) they change all the time, and (2) we can reinvent ourselves as whomever we want and whenever we want, as often as every single day. They're just words on a page, but we can turn them into actions and make them part of who we really are. *What will be your three words today?*

## reflections and intentions

my thoughts and feelings on today's FLASHPOINTS include:

my intentions and action items today include:

today I am grateful for:

# We can't solve problems by using the same kind of thinking we used when we created them.

~ Albert Einstein

Great leaders are innovators and forward-thinkers, opportunity-watchers and problem-solvers. However, sometimes we're so bogged down in our usual pattern of thinking that we can't see a better way of doing things. The solution? We need someone to help point us to a better or different way, which can quickly increase our problem-solving capability. If we regularly seek out the counsel of mentors, our capacity and perspective are enhanced. Rather than relying on our old habits, we'll be able to combine our usual approaches with new, novel ones. Success may still be ours without that trusted advisor, but with one … watch out, world! Humble yourself, ask for help, and prepare for great change. *What challenge are you facing that could improve with a fresh perspective?*

## reflections and intentions

my thoughts and feelings on today's FLASHPOINTS include:

my intentions and action items today include:

today I am grateful for:

## "Bless this mess," because it's not contributing to my success.

A clear desk, tidy inbox and well-planned appointment book are not just for the meticulously organized. Keeping our environment clutter-free allows room for clear thinking and new innovation. In much the same way that extra physical weight can make simple tasks harder, the messes in our lives put an extra strain on our productivity and creativity muscles. It's not just our inbox that is affected; it impacts every area in which we want to excel. Sometimes that mess seems overwhelming, and we wonder where the _____ we should even start. Simply pick one thing, dedicate 30 minutes to it each of the next five days, and watch what happens! *What one thing bothers you the most, that you will begin tackling in the next 24 hours?*

## reflections and intentions

my thoughts and feelings on today's FLASHPOINTS include:

my intentions and action items today include:

today I am grateful for:

# Teamwork divides the tasks and multiplies the success.

It's common knowledge that some of the most significant challenges in life can be overcome more easily with good ol' teamwork. After all, teamwork makes facing life's challenges a whole lot more fun! The truth is, we are born to interact with others ... at first with family, and then through life with friends, colleagues and community. In fact, most of the enjoyment in achieving anything worthwhile in life is in sharing it with others. Being part of a high-performing, super-achieving team is a life-changing experience ... a group of people, subscribed to the same vision, headed toward a shared goal, and experiencing unique interactions along the way is powerful and unforgettable. *Have you ever experienced the rush of high-octane teamwork? How can you create that experience for your team?*

## reflections and intentions

my thoughts and feelings on today's FLASHPOINTS include:

my intentions and action items today include:

today I am grateful for:

> ## Your most unhappy customers are your greatest source of learning.
> ### ~ Bill Gates

After five days of prompting and prodding new ideas and thoughts to come to mind, today we review what we've discovered. It's time to take a peek back at our journaling, to review our thoughts, feelings, and action items; and see how well we did. After all, self-awareness is the key to initiate growth and realize lasting change.

## weekly reflection

reflecting on my thoughts, feelings and experiences from this past week, the top three that impacted me the most include:

my top "ta-da's" (successes) from this past week include:

my top "oh-no's" (disappointments) from this past week include:

my top "ah-ha's" (discoveries) from this past week include:

> ## *There are only two ways to live your life. One is as though nothing is a miracle. The other is as though everything is a miracle.*
> ~ Albert Einstein

The end of the week is the best time to plan for the coming week. And at this point, you've reviewed the previous week and can be prepared to make changes and take actions based on thought, not re-action. You want to keep your goals in mind always. So today is your opportunity to look at yesterday's Weekly Reflection and decide what you're going to do and when. It is most often small tweaks that will lead to great success, fueled by a positive and grateful attitude.

## weekly intentions

my top "go get-'em's" (fixes) to implement this coming week include:

incomplete action items, that support my goals, to carry over into this coming week include: (schedule them now and be specific.)

new action items, that support my goals, for this coming week include: (schedule them now and be specific.)

something new I'm grateful for this week, and with whom I will share it:

## Remember, the last three letters in the word 'trend' are 'end.'

Trends end and fashions fade, but good style never goes away. Sure, we must be cunning and capitalize on trends, using them to draw attention to our brand, but it should never replace our core values. When establishing our personal, professional or corporate identity, focus less on what's hot and what's not, and more on the true and timeless image we want to portray. Remember, our image is formed in many ways: traditional iconography, branding and design, messaging, languaging, client interactions, and even the personalities of our teammates. Give careful consideration to how all these affect and form our image and turn down the emphasis on trends and fads. *How will you build a lasting identity that's true to your values ... trend or no trend?*

## reflections and intentions

my thoughts and feelings on today's FLASHPOINTS include:

my intentions and action items today include:

today I am grateful for:

# Fools tell friends what they want to hear.
# Mentors tell achievers what they need to hear.

From solopreneurs to industry titans, we all struggle with the tug of time that leaves little margin to find a mentor. It's easier than ever, however, to identify coaching programs that fit every budget and season of our lives. A simple internet search reveals business personalities, websites and blogs of every ilk dedicated to inspire success seekers with their programs, systems and strategies. Don't be fooled, however, by those salesy shysters who have a "system" to create wealth or success overnight … check references and do your homework! While it might take some time to find the appropriate mentor to join us on our journey, the time and heartache he or she will save us is worth its weight in … success. *What voices are you listening to?*

## reflections and intentions

my thoughts and feelings on today's FLASHPOINTS include:

my intentions and action items today include:

today I am grateful for:

# Fresh insight is as easy as the "action ABCs": Who, What, When, Where, How, and Why?

We've all learned different anecdotes that apply to taking action, and this one's an oldie but a goodie. When launching a project or idea or reaffirming the next steps forward, follow this easy structure to chart the course or tweak the direction: Who—who is involved, who should be enrolled, and who is the customer? *What*—describe the idea in a single detailed sentence. *When*—when will each step happen? Where—where will the idea first be realized? *How*—what steps are needed? *Why*—most importantly, why are we doing this project? Now use *When* and *How* to create or update the guiding checklist, and use *Why* to cheer everyone toward the goal. *On which project do you need to apply the action ABCs?*

## reflections and intentions

my thoughts and feelings on today's FLASHPOINTS include:

my intentions and action items today include:

today I am grateful for:

# There's just not enough time in the day for negativity, especially our own. So buckle up!

Inside the hearts and minds of every high achiever is the battle for supremacy between attitude and emotions. Our heads may say, "I can and *will* make it," ... but our emotions proclaim, "Who am I to do this?" Some days, that battle can be especially fierce, and the potential for giving up is particularly strong. We find ourselves rationalizing that, even though it might sting, quitting just short of the finish line would be the best thing to do. When those feelings of doubt and despair creep in, it's time to open the car window and toss our emotions along the side of the road. There's just no room in our Ferrari for the negativity passenger. *Who's reigning supreme in your battle for greatness, attitude or emotion?*

## reflections and intentions

my thoughts and feelings on today's FLASHPOINTS include:

my intentions and action items today include:

today I am grateful for:

## Compounding interest doesn't apply only to money.

As leaders and visionaries, we're obligated to create and foster an exciting and motivational environment for those in our charge. How do we best accomplish this? First, don't underestimate the power we have to inspire others simply by being inspired ourselves. Showing our enthusiasm and passion every day, in every way, spreads the motivational virus. If we haven't done this, stop reading now … before doing anything else, it's time to get reconnected with why we're leading. Second, rekindle the fire in others by sharing the foundational "why" stories that bond a team at the soul level. Beyond that, consider a timeout, a meeting somewhere other than the office, or an experiential bonding experience for your team. *Does the motivation, inspiration and excitement in your organization or project need a turbo boost?*

### reflections and intentions

my thoughts and feelings on today's FLASHPOINTS include:

my intentions and action items today include:

today I am grateful for:

> ## *Ordinary people think merely of spending time. Great people think of using it.*
>
> ### ~ Anonymous

After five days of prompting and prodding new ideas and thoughts to come to mind, today we review what we've discovered. It's time to take a peek back at our journaling, to review our thoughts, feelings, and action items; and see how well we did. After all, self-awareness is the key to initiate growth and realize lasting change.

## weekly reflection

reflecting on my thoughts, feelings and experiences from this past week, the top three that impacted me the most include:

my top "ta-da's" (successes) from this past week include:

my top "oh-no's" (disappointments) from this past week include:

my top "ah-ha's" (discoveries) from this past week include:

> ## Having a positive mental attitude is asking how something can be done rather than saying it can't be done.
> ### ~ Bo Bennett

The end of the week is the best time to plan for the coming week. And at this point, you've reviewed the previous week and can be prepared to make changes and take actions based on thought, not re-action. You want to keep your goals in mind always. So today is your opportunity to look at yesterday's Weekly Reflection and decide what you're going to do and when. It is most often small tweaks that will lead to great success, fueled by a positive and grateful attitude.

## weekly intentions

my top "go get-'em's" (fixes) to implement this coming week include:

incomplete action items, that support my goals, to carry over into this coming week include: (schedule them now and be specific.)

new action items, that support my goals, for this coming week include: (schedule them now and be specific.)

something new I'm grateful for this week, and with whom I will share it:

## The more audacious the goal, the more flexibility required.

When we commit to a mind-blowing goal, we must accept that it likely won't be achieved overnight. The longer it takes, the more likely it is that we'll deviate from our plan over time because of changes in market conditions, team members, resources or client feedback. But what should we do when straying from the path wasn't intentional, and it seems like we've lost our way? Begin by reflecting on whether our original vision is still relevant and important to us. No matter our findings, an infusion of fresh ideas is necessary so we can *purposefully* and *passionately* strive toward something bigger than ourselves. Action plans are simply guides that continually need adjustments. *What course corrections do you need to make to get closer to your valued visions?*

## reflections and intentions

my thoughts and feelings on today's FLASHPOINTS include:

my intentions and action items today include:

today I am grateful for:

# What are you doing?!

No matter what we do, whether starting a business, keeping a job, volunteering, running the local marathon or for public office, people will judge our motivations. Here's the good news: their opinions don't mean squat. Some things we do out of love ... other things, to sustain a lifestyle. When we live with intentionality, we get the chance to change the world *and* earn a comfortable living while doing it. What matters is being honest with ourselves about our motivations, because eventually they'll be obvious to everyone else, too. Why not start being truthful about them right here, right now? Do you measure your impact in dollars, accomplishments, or testimonials from others? Are you driven by ego, revenge and cash, or legacy and changed lives? *Why do you do what you do?*

## reflections and intentions

my thoughts and feelings on today's FLASHPOINTS include:

my intentions and action items today include:

today I am grateful for:

# Motivating ourselves is addition; motivating our team is multiplication!

We, rightly, work hard to maintain our daily motivation. But we should work harder to motivate others. A 20% gain in productivity for each person of a team of 10 is greater than a 40% gain for ourselves! And when it comes down to it, what motivates us is the same that motivates others: competition, weekly targets, incentives, recognition, a sense of mission, etc. As Daniel Pink states in his book "Motivation", we all need three key elements: autonomy (control over our environment), mastery (a sense we're progressively becoming better), and purpose (something beyond ourselves to shoot for). Understand how each person can achieve these things from their contribution, and new life will be breathed into their work. *What can you do to provide more motivation to yourself and others?*

## reflections and intentions

my thoughts and feelings on today's FLASHPOINTS include:

my intentions and action items today include:

today I am grateful for:

## Take, take, take ...
## lessons aren't given, they're taken.

When developing professional relationships, it's common to surround ourselves with people like ourselves. That is, people who are enterprising, passionate and motivated and who share our core values. This should also be true for our mentors ... but, let's not get seduced into surrounding ourselves with a bunch of "mini-mes." Our mentoring relationships should include folks who stretch and challenge us intellectually and professionally ... insight and innovation are born of different perspectives. Inherent in the pursuit of excellence is the understanding that pain, learning and growth will be the byproduct. So, while it's important to build a relationship with a mentor we trust, respect and admire, we should be looking for diversity in background, experience and perspective. *What lesson have you learned from someone bolder and brighter this week?*

## reflections and intentions

my thoughts and feelings on today's FLASHPOINTS include:

my intentions and action items today include:

today I am grateful for:

## Just because it's small doesn't mean it's child's play.

The little things we do each day—every email, solution, conversation, reaction, meeting, or presentation—are all opportunities to impress, achieve and succeed. While we may be aiming for stellar performance at the big client meeting or on a major final exam, it's the small things done each day in preparation that lead to success. If we truly care enough about the *big* thing, we'll take comfort in knowing success comes with taking care of the *little* things ... and we'll experience joy in them. So, recognize the big opportunity that lays ahead, then break it down into minor opportunities and perform with excellence over and over again. *What small things have you been avoiding (or offering less than your best) that impact your quest for greatness?*

## reflections and intentions

my thoughts and feelings on today's FLASHPOINTS include:

my intentions and action items today include:

today I am grateful for:

> # Some people forget to plant in the spring, idle away the summer hours and then expect to reap in the fall.
>
> ## ~ Anonymous

After five days of prompting and prodding new ideas and thoughts to come to mind, today we review what we've discovered. It's time to take a peek back at our journaling, to review our thoughts, feelings, and action items; and see how well we did. After all, self-awareness is the key to initiate growth and realize lasting change.

## weekly reflection

reflecting on my thoughts, feelings and experiences from this past week, the top three that impacted me the most include:

my top "ta-da's" (successes) from this past week include:

my top "oh-no's" (disappointments) from this past week include:

my top "ah-ha's" (discoveries) from this past week include:

## A man grows most tired while standing still.

~ Chinese Proverb

The end of the week is the best time to plan for the coming week. And at this point, you've reviewed the previous week and can be prepared to make changes and take actions based on thought, not re-action. You want to keep your goals in mind always. So today is your opportunity to look at yesterday's Weekly Reflection and decide what you're going to do and when. It is most often small tweaks that will lead to great success, fueled by a positive and grateful attitude.

## weekly intentions

my top "go get-'em's" (fixes) to implement this coming week include:

incomplete action items, that support my goals, to carry over into this coming week include: (schedule them now and be specific.)

new action items, that support my goals, for this coming week include: (schedule them now and be specific.)

something new I'm grateful for this week, and with whom I will share it:

FLASHPOINTS for achievers

## Slooow down ....
## and enjoy the realization of
## milestones along the way.

We've all been challenged to reflect on how we'll know when we've "made it," when we've achieved what we set out to do in our business, community and personal ventures. Equally important is recognizing small successes along the way, which contribute to edging us closer to our ultimate goal. Taking time out to celebrate milestones can be the opportunity for a personal acknowledgment, a season of thanksgiving and inspiration. Best of all, use these opportunities to reward our stakeholders as well; what a perfect opportunity to foster cohesion among those in our sphere of influence. *When was the last time you paused to celebrate a milestone with your team?*

## reflections and intentions

my thoughts and feelings on today's FLASHPOINTS include:

my intentions and action items today include:

today I am grateful for:

# What's good for the goose may NOT be good for the gander.

In life, everything is relative to our personal goals and experiences ... a small expense for some might be totally extravagant for others. Except it really isn't about the expense—it's about the *value* of the resulting experience. The same is true when taking action to achieve our goals. What might be bold and reckless for some might be baby steps for others. The resulting experience that the action can produce, how deep the desire is and the potential value gained are what will drive us forward, no matter how much our ego gets battered and bloodied. One thing's for sure: if what drives us to take daily action is something worth fighting for, the fight becomes much easier. *Can you articulate the value of what you're fighting for?*

## reflections and intentions

my thoughts and feelings on today's FLASHPOINTS include:

my intentions and action items today include:

today I am grateful for:

## Fitness coach to client: "Just show up." Say what?

I overheard a fitness coach giving that advice on how much exercise we should be doing. Interestingly, the same can be applied to leadership and achievement in most areas of our professional and personal lives. There are days when we're full of energy, ideas and enthusiasm; concern for others; and, we can't wait to get going. Then there are days when we're tired and stressed; an unexpected crisis rears its ugly head, and we're tempted to run the other way. These become our make-or-break times. Times to "just show up" and be present with those in need. Effective leadership isn't just about speed, power and accomplishment; it's about doing what's needed, even when we don't feel like it. *Where should you "just show up" this week?*

### reflections and intentions

my thoughts and feelings on today's FLASHPOINTS include:

my intentions and action items today include:

today I am grateful for:

## Authenticity has no competition.

Authenticity and transparency are requirements for powerful, transformational leadership in our new *Relationship Economy*. Undoubtedly, to inspire and evoke passion among our team members and stakeholders, our vision statement *must* be authentic. This can only happen if our vision is clear, truthful, well formed, and straightforward, without relying on pompous or flowery phrases. Focus exactly on what the business or project is meant to bring about in the world, capture it in as few words as possible, and keep those words simple enough for a child to understand. Don't forget that our vision for significant impact is what team members at every level of the organization will aspire to achieve, so it must to be genuine, inspiring, and uncomplicated. *How can your vision statement be more pure?*

### reflections and intentions

my thoughts and feelings on today's FLASHPOINTS include:

my intentions and action items today include:

today I am grateful for:

## Imagine a hidden camera recording your business or life. What would the footage show?

Social media provides us with quick ways to spread stories and videos like never before. When a business is found skimping on value, service or delivery, word spreads like wildfire. A worldwide delivery service was shown in poor form when home videos surfaced, showing the mishandling of their customer's parcels. The footage posed important questions for consumers, such as "What are the businesses that support me even when I'm not looking?" Sometimes any publicity is good publicity, but that's a high-risk strategy. It's better to be proactive and use our own "hidden cameras" to uncover glaring areas of underperformance. Our customers will definitely appreciate that. And so will we. *What would a hidden camera reveal about your life or business?*

## reflections and intentions

my thoughts and feelings on today's FLASHPOINTS include:

my intentions and action items today include:

today I am grateful for:

## Remember the turtle - He never makes any progress 'til he sticks his neck out.
~ Anonymous

After five days of prompting and prodding new ideas and thoughts to come to mind, today we review what we've discovered. It's time to take a peek back at our journaling, to review our thoughts, feelings, and action items; and see how well we did. After all, self-awareness is the key to initiate growth and realize lasting change.

## weekly reflection

reflecting on my thoughts, feelings and experiences from this past week, the top three that impacted me the most include:

my top "ta-da's" (successes) from this past week include:

my top "oh-no's" (disappointments) from this past week include:

my top "ah-ha's" (discoveries) from this past week include:

> # A winner is someone who recognizes his God-given talents, works his tail off to develop them into skills and uses these skills to accomplish his goals.
>
> ## ~ Larry Bird

The end of the week is the best time to plan for the coming week. And at this point, you've reviewed the previous week and can be prepared to make changes and take actions based on thought, not re-action. You want to keep your goals in mind always. So today is your opportunity to look at yesterday's Weekly Reflection and decide what you're going to do and when. It is most often small tweaks that will lead to great success, fueled by a positive and grateful attitude.

## weekly intentions

my top "go get-'em's" (fixes) to implement this coming week include:

incomplete action items, that support my goals, to carry over into this coming week include: (schedule them now and be specific.)

new action items, that support my goals, for this coming week include: (schedule them now and be specific.)

something new I'm grateful for this week, and with whom I will share it:

# Legacies are built not by accepting favors but by performing them.

Whether formally or informally, we've all benefited from a mentor at some stage in our lives. Perhaps it was a teacher, a parent, pastor, business colleague or simply a friend. It might have been in the form of great advice, a listening ear, an encouraging word, unconditional love or just the bonding of two peers sharing common interests and ideas and providing feedback to each other. While all of these situations are eye-opening for us, and it's nice to be poured into by someone, it's just as rewarding to be the one offering the mentoring. There are folks in our sphere of influence who'd appreciate learning from our experience, and would greatly value our input. *To whom can you "pay it forward" to this week ... or even this month?*

## reflections and intentions

my thoughts and feelings on today's FLASHPOINTS include:

my intentions and action items today include:

today I am grateful for:

## Our weakness can improve our strengths, if we use it in the right way.

Ah, the shellacking we give ourselves for procrastination. Those times when we give in to weakness and wasted precious time. It's Facebook, Twitter, or the latest gaming forums or business blogs ... whatever thief we allow to steal our time. How can we actually take advantage of this weakness? By turning it into a reward system! We can treat ourselves to engaging in this activity when we've completed a certain portion of our to-do list. Take an unpleasant task that cannot be deferred, give it your full attention for a solid hour, then reward yourself with the guilty pleasure of 15 minutes of procrastination! Giving ourselves permission to indulge can work to our advantage if we use it judiciously. *How can you turn your weakness into a motivator?*

### reflections and intentions

my thoughts and feelings on today's FLASHPOINTS include:

my intentions and action items today include:

today I am grateful for:

# Don't underestimate the intelligence of a crowd.

Crowdsourcing is the practice of inviting the wider community to get involved in our project or business, either through collaboration or competition. Let's say we are looking to name or improve our latest product—put it to the public and invite them to vote to help decide. Think about the successful introduction of blue M&Ms, Doritos Super Bowl ads, and 99designs; or consider the wide range of crowdfunding sites to see if what we're doing resonates with consumers or stakeholders. Why harness the brainpower of just a few when there's the potential to engage thousands? While there are pros and cons to crowdsourcing, it's very possible that our next project is a perfect fit. *What part of your plan can you delegate to the crowds?*

## reflections and intentions

my thoughts and feelings on today's FLASHPOINTS include:

my intentions and action items today include:

today I am grateful for:

## Never take the back seat— unless you're willing to let someone else take the wheel and steer for you.

We get first shot at deciding which direction we take in life—in our careers, personal lives, health, relationships, education and more. We may have chosen to let someone else decide our path, but don't be mistaken: *it was still our choice.* We don't need to continually travel through life on the suggestions of others. We don't have to be a product of our circumstances; we can choose to change and become a product of our *own* choices. Being proactive and taking action is paramount if we want to do things our own way. This means we need to get in the driver's seat, take control of the wheel and step on the gas. *How are you taking charge to create the kind of life you want?*

## reflections and intentions

my thoughts and feelings on today's FLASHPOINTS include:

my intentions and action items today include:

today I am grateful for:

## *Multiplicity* may be just a B-movie, but there's an important lesson in it for us.

Most leaders and high achievers strive toward a mission of enduring value, inspiration and legacy that's bigger than themselves. It's important we remember that our own leadership role is rarely permanent when building legacy, but it's critical now for the ultimate success of our mission. Doesn't it make sense, then, to "clone" ourselves in some fashion, to avoid organizational collapse? While modern science isn't regularly cloning humans, there's nothing stopping us from creating our own heir apparent right now. What if the best and brightest on the team were given the opportunity and coaching to continue our legacy, as leaders in their own right? That's the start of building a succession plan, and it's thinking with the end in mind. *Whom on your team would you consider elevating, and why?*

## reflections and intentions

my thoughts and feelings on today's FLASHPOINTS include:

my intentions and action items today include:

today I am grateful for:

> # Be like a postage stamp.
> # Stick to it until you get there.
> ### ~ Harvey Mackay

After five days of prompting and prodding new ideas and thoughts to come to mind, today we review what we've discovered. It's time to take a peek back at our journaling, to review our thoughts, feelings, and action items; and see how well we did. After all, self-awareness is the key to initiate growth and realize lasting change.

## weekly reflection

reflecting on my thoughts, feelings and experiences from this past week, the top three that impacted me the most include:

my top "ta-da's" (successes) from this past week include:

my top "oh-no's" (disappointments) from this past week include:

my top "ah-ha's" (discoveries) from this past week include:

> ## The great thing in the world is not so much where we stand, as in what direction we are moving.
> ~ Oliver Wendell Holmes Jr.

The end of the week is the best time to plan for the coming week. And at this point, you've reviewed the previous week and can be prepared to make changes and take actions based on thought, not re-action. You want to keep your goals in mind always. So today is your opportunity to look at yesterday's Weekly Reflection and decide what you're going to do and when. It is most often small tweaks that will lead to great success, fueled by a positive and grateful attitude.

## weekly intentions

my top "go get-'em's" (fixes) to implement this coming week include:

incomplete action items, that support my goals, to carry over into this coming week include: (schedule them now and be specific.)

new action items, that support my goals, for this coming week include: (schedule them now and be specific.)

something new I'm grateful for this week, and with whom I will share it:

> # Our work is to discover our work and then, with all our heart, give ourselves to it.

When we want to learn, develop, and kick some professional booty, we usually look outward to resources such as books, websites, seminars, podcasts, and teachers. We naturally do this when we're searching for answers. Yet, when it's time for personal growth and enlightenment to discover our passion and purpose, we turn our attention inward for serious reflection and contemplation. After a provocative mountaintop transformation experience, or perhaps just some edification and refinement, we cast our search outward again to get to know ourselves even better. Here's how we do that: meet new people and glean insight from their trials, triumphs and even their FLASHPOINTS stories. That perspective may be just what's needed to recognize our purpose and realize our fullest potential. *Where will you look next for clarity and inspiration?*

## reflections and intentions

my thoughts and feelings on today's FLASHPOINTS include:

my intentions and action items today include:

today I am grateful for:

# When on fire, we know to stop, drop, and roll. In life, we must stop, drop, and reflect.

Reflection could be the most underrated resource in our lives, businesses, and projects. It may not take much *time* to "take five" to quiet our minds and unwind after a stressful day or interaction or to ask our clients and stakeholders how things are going, but it does take *effort*. It's easy to postpone this critical task, instead focusing on the urgent matters that vie for our attention. Regular reflection and introspection, however, provides the opportunity to fine-tune our thoughts, communications, relationships, products and services, which leads to increased confidence that our efforts are bringing value to those we love and serve. The only thing worse than being misunderstood or missing the mark is not even *knowing* it. *What project or area of your life requires additional reflection and introspection?*

## reflections and intentions

my thoughts and feelings on today's FLASHPOINTS include:

my intentions and action items today include:

today I am grateful for:

# Progress, not perfection.

As savvy, educated and open-minded individuals, we're *always* looking for ways to improve, embrace, and grow. From our interactions with others, to our presentation skills, to our understanding of our craft, it's all about getting better. Since perfection is unattainable, how do we know we've reached our peak? That's the fun part—we never do! Yet it's important for us to know we're on the right path. To do that, we need to give our ultimate dedication and focus to every task. And it doesn't require winning a medal or award; it means that even if our outreach is only small, we've exceeded the expectations of the folks we're affecting. And that includes us. *What is going on in your life that could use some increased focus and perseverance?*

## reflections and intentions

my thoughts and feelings on today's FLASHPOINTS include:

my intentions and action items today include:

today I am grateful for:

## Strengths unused or unknown might as well be weaknesses.

We lead by example, take bold steps and delight in taking ourselves, our teams and our business/project to new heights, right? We engage in a relationship with mentors to harness their strengths and experiences; and when we have an optimal bond with them, we end up learning more about ourselves then we ever imagined possible. This ally can truthfully tell us what they see in us and our business/project, both strengths and weaknesses, which not only confirms what we know about ourselves but will surprise us with what we don't know. If the relationship is healthy, they'll see some of themselves in us and can help us leverage those strengths of greater good. *List your strengths. How do you know that's all you have? Go ask your mentor.*

## reflections and intentions

my thoughts and feelings on today's FLASHPOINTS include:

my intentions and action items today include:

today I am grateful for:

## Team building is like deep sea diving: the deeper we go, the more pressure we feel.

The performance of high-functioning teams rely on a multitude of factors. Gone are the days when a simple dose of team-building activities (like Trust Falls and Manifestation Circles) would restore productivity. (Did those days ever really exist?) Although team building games have their place, relying on them to solve deeply rooted problems could mask significant issues and thus yield few sustainable results. A decline in team productivity or morale could be symptomatic of an underlying problem that requires greater analysis. Perhaps it's a lack of direction, purpose, leadership or resources. Finding that source, however, isn't for surface-dwellers ... we must be prepared to go deep, remain open-minded, listen intently and then DO something about it! *How would you rate your team's productivity and performance? Should you take a deeper dive?*

### reflections and intentions

my thoughts and feelings on today's FLASHPOINTS include:

my intentions and action items today include:

today I am grateful for:

> ## The difference between greatness and mediocrity is often how an individual views a mistake.
>
> ~ Nelson Boswell

After five days of prompting and prodding new ideas and thoughts to come to mind, today we review what we've discovered. It's time to take a peek back at our journaling, to review our thoughts, feelings, and action items; and see how well we did. After all, self-awareness is the key to initiate growth and realize lasting change.

## weekly reflection

reflecting on my thoughts, feelings and experiences from this past week, the top three that impacted me the most include:

my top "ta-da's" (successes) from this past week include:

my top "oh-no's" (disappointments) from this past week include:

my top "ah-ha's" (discoveries) from this past week include:

> ## A hero is no braver than an ordinary man, but he is braver five minutes longer.
> ### ~ Ralph Waldo Emerson

The end of the week is the best time to plan for the coming week. And at this point, you've reviewed the previous week and can be prepared to make changes and take actions based on thought, not re-action. You want to keep your goals in mind always. So today is your opportunity to look at yesterday's Weekly Reflection and decide what you're going to do and when. It is most often small tweaks that will lead to great success, fueled by a positive and grateful attitude.

## weekly intentions

my top "go get-'em's" (fixes) to implement this coming week include:

incomplete action items, that support my goals, to carry over into this coming week include: (schedule them now and be specific.)

new action items, that support my goals, for this coming week include: (schedule them now and be specific.)

something new I'm grateful for this week, and with whom I will share it:

# We can't always get we we want ...
# but when we look inside,
# we very likely already have it.

It's so easy to get on the toxic train of thinking that we just need something else to succeed. We start saying to ourselves, "If I just had X, Y or Z, I'd be successful!" Then, of course, we secure X, Y or Z, and then it's A, B or C holding us back. We're all guilty of accumulating the next great tool, the latest diet or the next conference that promises success. Sometimes they can help, but they aren't necessary. Entrepreneurs are amazingly resourceful ... people in the heart of Africa show us we've already got what it takes after getting basics like clean water, a little capital and a market need. It's done with exactly this: *ourselves. How can you use what you already have to succeed now?*

## reflections and intentions

my thoughts and feelings on today's FLASHPOINTS include:

my intentions and action items today include:

today I am grateful for:

# Make your life about the other people in it.

At the core of many great leaders throughout history is the concept of servant leadership. This concept encourages leaders to lead by being of service to their team members. When our role exists to be of service to others by supporting and developing them, we bring out the best in those on our team ... and team member gratitude, productivity and loyalty skyrocket as a result. As an added bonus, it's absolutely rewarding to see folks move closer to their fullest potential while in our charge. When contemplating the leadership strategies we hope to deploy, its helpful to think of leaders we admire most: what qualities, traits and values do/did they possess? *How will history define your leadership legacy?*

## reflections and intentions

my thoughts and feelings on today's FLASHPOINTS include:

my intentions and action items today include:

today I am grateful for:

# Strategy vs. Vision
# What's the deal?

As we're contemplating our vision, we're often tempted to skip straight to strategy. We start asking ourselves, "How can we make it all happen?" Before diving into that question, we've got to remember it's likely that the ideas themselves need more developing. And while we're thinking further on that idea, a better and faster path may appear. Be specific: it's not just about the goal but the team we'll need to create to begin the attack, the value-filters we must apply and the desired timeframe for it all. So before jumping into strategy, take a few minutes to shed new light on the idea. *Is your vision ready for strategy, or do you need to think a little longer on it?*

## reflections and intentions

my thoughts and feelings on today's FLASHPOINTS include:

my intentions and action items today include:

today I am grateful for:

> # If the work you do isn't worth collating and highlighting, you probably need to be doing better work.
> ### ~ Seth Godin

With our never-ending task list, we're so busy that we often just want to get that piece of work out the door and move on. There's a time for that, but there's also a time to make that piece of work a piece of *art*. What's the use in offering up mediocrity when we know we can create a masterpiece? The good news is that *excellence* doesn't always require crazy *effort* … just a final walk-through or review from a trusted, artistic colleague will do the trick. We'd much rather look back on a history of work we can take pride in than half-baked efforts to be forgotten. Seth's right: do your work as if it will be in a museum someday. *What does your work history say about you?*

## reflections and intentions

my thoughts and feelings on today's FLASHPOINTS include:

my intentions and action items today include:

today I am grateful for:

## The key to success is to never stop learning. The key to failure is to think we know it all.

Nothing is more hazardous to an achiever's success than to stop taking in new information and ideas ... just like us, the world is constantly evolving. That's why it's always best to say, "Thanks for the reminder, tell me more," rather than, "I already know that." When we invite people to share their wisdom and knowledge (rather than blocking it), we'll enrich our own lives ... and guess what? The next ground-breaking idea might just organically spring from within! When we drop our defenses and embrace the attitude, "I can learn from anyone," we start accepting mentoring from everyone. Formal mentoring relationships are critical, but why limit ourselves to those interactions? Are you willing to learn from each person you meet today? *Use the phrase, "Tell me more."*

## reflections and intentions

my thoughts and feelings on today's FLASHPOINTS include:

my intentions and action items today include:

today I am grateful for:

> # *If you're coasting, you're either losing momentum or else you're headed downhill.*
>
> ### ~ Joan Welsh

After five days of prompting and prodding new ideas and thoughts to come to mind, today we review what we've discovered. It's time to take a peek back at our journaling, to review our thoughts, feelings, and action items; and see how well we did. After all, self-awareness is the key to initiate growth and realize lasting change.

## weekly reflection

reflecting on my thoughts, feelings and experiences from this past week, the top three that impacted me the most include:

my top "ta-da's" (successes) from this past week include:

my top "oh-no's" (disappointments) from this past week include:

my top "ah-ha's" (discoveries) from this past week include:

> # The quality of a person's life is in direct proportion to their commitment to excellence, regardless of their chosen field of endeavor.
>
> ~ Vince Lombardi

The end of the week is the best time to plan for the coming week. And at this point, you've reviewed the previous week and can be prepared to make changes and take actions based on thought, not re-action. You want to keep your goals in mind always. So today is your opportunity to look at yesterday's Weekly Reflection and decide what you're going to do and when. It is most often small tweaks that will lead to great success, fueled by a positive and grateful attitude.

## weekly intentions

my top "go get-'em's" (fixes) to implement this coming week include:

incomplete action items, that support my goals, to carry over into this coming week include: (schedule them now and be specific.)

new action items, that support my goals, for this coming week include: (schedule them now and be specific.)

something new I'm grateful for this week, and with whom I will share it:

## Burnout is the world's way of telling us we're disconnected from our purpose and calling.

It's vital not to ignore this message. We aren't built for continuously driving ourselves 100 miles an hour, like a race car. Even if we're passionate about our ideas and projects, we can become burnt out or bored if we don't take an occasional breather. Elite athletes have an offseason; schools have extended breaks; even God rested on the 7th day! So let's do the same … our bodies, our brains and our families need it. Slowing down to rest and reflect offers time and space to appreciate what we've accomplished and brings creativity and perspective to help recognize how we can improve things further. When was the last time you treated yourself to a little R & R? *How will you make it a regular part of your achievement cycle?*

## reflections and intentions

my thoughts and feelings on today's FLASHPOINTS include:

my intentions and action items today include:

today I am grateful for:

# Play is more fun than work!

I read somewhere that by the age of twenty one, the average millennial will have spent 10,000 hours playing video games ... for us older folks, we shout in glorious victory when we get in the fastest moving checkout line! Why? We all enjoy the challenge and the reward of competition. According to game designer Jane McGonigal, the positive traits that gamers develop include: the drive for productivity, "urgent optimism" and the ability to "weave a tight social fabric." Sounds like great attributes for any high-functioning team! And so enters the concept of gamification: since gaming is here to stay, doesn't it make sense that we apply the dynamics of a game to a non-game environment to reap the benefits of increased stimulation? *How can you apply gamification to your team?*

## reflections and intentions

my thoughts and feelings on today's FLASHPOINTS include:

my intentions and action items today include:

today I am grateful for:

> # In preparing for battle I have always found that plans are useless, but planning is indispensable.
>
> ~ Dwight Eisenhower

When it comes to taking action, an overly elaborate plan can be just as crippling as having no plan ... it's not only the time spent forming the intricate plan, but also the complexity of its execution. Simply recognizing there's so much to do and so little time can throw us into a panic and make us want to quit. Since no plan survives contact with the enemy, it's best we K.I.S.S. When, *not if*, our plan falls apart, it's much easier to make course corrections along the way. Start with just a few steps and lean toward more detail for immediate actions and less detail for what comes later. When in doubt, simplify! *Where in your planning do you need to simplify or make course corrections?*

## reflections and intentions

my thoughts and feelings on today's FLASHPOINTS include:

my intentions and action items today include:

today I am grateful for:

## Are entrepreneurs the modern-day anti-hero?

In a world full of excelling individuals and advances in technology faster than you can say "3D printing," the emphasis is no longer on growing up to become a superhero. Why? It's simple: we no longer dream about developing super powers to achieve the extraordinary. Instead, our hearts are set on achieving the impossible sans-kryptonite, and it's happening everywhere we look. That's right, we're human, we're flawed and, although we can't scale tall buildings in a single bound, here's what we CAN do: dream, innovate and problem solve like never before. Now I know we all wish for a little magic sometimes, like x-ray vision or time travel abilities, but there's almost unlimited power in just being human. *What do you need to do to let your inner super-hero loose?*

## reflections and intentions

my thoughts and feelings on today's FLASHPOINTS include:

my intentions and action items today include:

today I am grateful for:

> # We can do almost anything, but we can't do everything.

High achievers tend to want it all and actually believe we can do it all. We often say "yes" to so many worthy causes,; however, with that, we get lost in the sea of good intentions and lose sight of the shoreline of accomplishments meant to propel our favorite cause toward greatness. We spread our time, attentions and intentions so thin that we open the door to mediocrity. There's an endless supply of problems, people and causes vying for our talents and attentions, so we must identify the ones that mean the most to us … and guard against the others by defining our boundaries and defending our borders. *Identify three problems, causes, and organizations that deserve your time, talent, energy and emotion. Now what are you going to do?*

## reflections and intentions

my thoughts and feelings on today's FLASHPOINTS include:

my intentions and action items today include:

today I am grateful for:

> # *Being rich is having money; being wealthy is having time.*
> ### ~ Margaret Bonnano

After five days of prompting and prodding new ideas and thoughts to come to mind, today we review what we've discovered. It's time to take a peek back at our journaling, to review our thoughts, feelings, and action items; and see how well we did. After all, self-awareness is the key to initiate growth and realize lasting change.

## weekly reflection

reflecting on my thoughts, feelings and experiences from this past week, the top three that impacted me the most include:

my top "ta-da's" (successes) from this past week include:

my top "oh-no's" (disappointments) from this past week include:

my top "ah-ha's" (discoveries) from this past week include:

> ## *Our opinions become fixed at the point where we stop thinking.*
> ### ~ Ernest Renan

The end of the week is the best time to plan for the coming week. And at this point, you've reviewed the previous week and can be prepared to make changes and take actions based on thought, not re-action. You want to keep your goals in mind always. So today is your opportunity to look at yesterday's Weekly Reflection and decide what you're going to do and when. It is most often small tweaks that will lead to great success, fueled by a positive and grateful attitude.

## weekly intentions

my top "go get-'em's" (fixes) to implement this coming week include:

incomplete action items, that support my goals, to carry over into this coming week include: (schedule them now and be specific.)

new action items, that support my goals, for this coming week include: (schedule them now and be specific.)

something new I'm grateful for this week, and with whom I will share it:

# Don't stop talking about your ideas.

Even at the risk of sounding like a broken record, the best way to move our ideas forward is to talk about them ... with everyone. If something is important and we're really passionate about it, it makes sense for others to know about it, which means talking about it *constantly*. And the truth is, people really like to hear about our desires and dreams. It makes people happy to know that someone is striving for something big—it pumps them up, too! Don't be selective; we need to simply share with everyone we know what's on our minds and our to-do list. Who knows what kind of opportunities may open up or whom that person knows? *Who else can you share your ideas with today?*

## reflections and intentions

my thoughts and feelings on today's FLASHPOINTS include:

my intentions and action items today include:

today I am grateful for:

## Don't play *Follow The Leader;* instead, play *Catch Me If You Can.*

When playing in the big leagues of business, it can be a challenging to walk among the shadows of industry titans. Sometimes, it seems we're forced to follow in their footsteps and do as they do to improve awareness and market share of our product or service. We're often tempted to take action by following a similar path, releasing a similar product, or even running a similar marketing campaign—because, hey, if it worked for them, it should work for us, right? Wrong! This is where practicing innovation will set us on our own path to living a life of significance. Focus less on competing, and more on collaborating—and do things your way. *Are you playing Follow The Leader or Catch Me If You Can?*

## reflections and intentions

my thoughts and feelings on today's FLASHPOINTS include:

my intentions and action items today include:

today I am grateful for:

# There's a thin line between love and hate.

On any team—sports, business, family, volunteer—there's a thin line between *challenge* and pressure to perform at peak capacity. Limited challenges and low expectations usually lead to lackluster and stagnant team performance. With seemingly insurmountable challenge and overwhelming pressure, however, temptation mounts to just get the job done, ignoring unsafe or dangerous work conditions and neglecting opportunities for professional growth. From time to time, for even the most seasoned leaders, recognizing the location of this line is often difficult. The key is to seek regular input from our teams about their workload relative to the pending challenge … ask them to judge and report when performance expectations become *quantitative* instead of *qualitative*. *Are you challenging your team toward continual growth or pressuring them for performance?*

## reflections and intentions

my thoughts and feelings on today's FLASHPOINTS include:

my intentions and action items today include:

today I am grateful for:

> # Regardless of style, effective leaders follow the teachings of the great ones who have gone before us.

No matter where we are on the leadership spectrum, there's much to be learned from transformational leaders who've already succeeded. For example, Nelson Mandela shared some of the most foundational and uplifting leadership principles around. They're foundational because any leadership style can be furthered with them. Mandela teaches us that courage is NOT the absence of fear, and not just action in fear's presence, but the capability to inspire others to move beyond fear and into what smashes fear: *action.* He reminds us that when we lead from the front, we need some focus on those behind; when we lead from the back, we're to encourage others to embrace the front. *How do you deal with fear, and how do you inspire and lead those around you?*

## reflections and intentions

my thoughts and feelings on today's FLASHPOINTS include:

my intentions and action items today include:

today I am grateful for:

> ## They can take our lives,
> ## but they will never take our FREEDOM!
> ### ~ William Wallace

It's challenging for some of us (particularly, the highly analytical types) to invest in a lofty vision because, ultimately, there's nothing to suggest it's even possible to achieve it ... except our own burning desire. But is that enough? Maybe. When you think about it, history is filled with the realities of men and women who have fought bloodbaths for causes and lifestyles without any guarantee of ever seeing their vision fulfilled. The sheer audacity to realize that vision was enough for them to push on. Ultimately, the dreaming, the forging ahead, the dogged persistence was enough, regardless of the outcome. If the vision for our lives isn't like that and perhaps it's time for a change. *What inspires you to drive on toward your vision no matter what the outcome is?*

## reflections and intentions

my thoughts and feelings on today's FLASHPOINTS include:

my intentions and action items today include:

today I am grateful for:

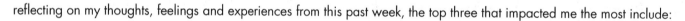

*The real voyage of discovery consists
not in seeking new landscapes,
but in having new eyes.*

~ Marcel Proust

After five days of prompting and prodding new ideas and thoughts to come to mind, today we review what we've discovered. It's time to take a peek back at our journaling, to review our thoughts, feelings, and action items; and see how well we did. After all, self-awareness is the key to initiate growth and realize lasting change.

## weekly reflection

reflecting on my thoughts, feelings and experiences from this past week, the top three that impacted me the most include:

my top "ta-da's" (successes) from this past week include:

my top "oh-no's" (disappointments) from this past week include:

my top "ah-ha's" (discoveries) from this past week include:

> ## Your next level of excellence is hidden behind your next level of resistance.
> ### ~ Robin Sharma

The end of the week is the best time to plan for the coming week. And at this point, you've reviewed the previous week and can be prepared to make changes and take actions based on thought, not re-action. You want to keep your goals in mind always. So today is your opportunity to look at yesterday's Weekly Reflection and decide what you're going to do and when. It is most often small tweaks that will lead to great success, fueled by a positive and grateful attitude.

## weekly intentions

my top "go get-'em's" (fixes) to implement this coming week include:

incomplete action items, that support my goals, to carry over into this coming week include: (schedule them now and be specific.)

new action items, that support my goals, for this coming week include: (schedule them now and be specific.)

something new I'm grateful for this week, and with whom I will share it:

## Living.
## It's a dirty job, but somebody's got to do it.

The path to significance is not always fun and games; it requires bold action, which means getting our hands dirty. It's about wholeheartedly *giving* all of ourselves to the challenge, because extraordinary *living* takes 100% effort. Here's what *actually* happens: we *think* about what we want to accomplish, our brain shifts into safety mode and tells us what could go wrong … suddenly we're not as excited, and our progress is stalled. Here's what *should* happen: we think of what we want to accomplish, our brains tell us what could go wrong … and *we decide to face the uncertainty head on.* Moving past our fears requires recognizing and accepting the feelings associated with the down side and *taking action anyway! How well do you embrace your fear of failure?*

## reflections and intentions

my thoughts and feelings on today's FLASHPOINTS include:

my intentions and action items today include:

today I am grateful for:

# The worst part of self-censorship is *@$%!

With clients, colleagues, employees and even ourselves, we scale and edit our inner thoughts over and over again, before releasing them … just look at what we do when writing blog entries or Facebook status updates. But if we've edited our original ideas so much that they barely resemble what we began with, are we really being true to ourselves? While we must exercise some level of proofreading and consideration of our readers, we can go too far the other way, watering down our thoughts so that they're diluted. The end result? *Zero impact.* And then, we've not only thrown any semblance of authenticity out the window, but wasted everyone's time. *In what areas of life are you diluting and editing out the true you?*

## reflections and intentions

my thoughts and feelings on today's FLASHPOINTS include:

my intentions and action items today include:

today I am grateful for:

> ## Work hard at your job and you can make a living. Work hard on yourself and you can make a fortune.
> ### ~ Jim Rohn

The key words here: "work" and "yourself." No matter what level of success we've obtained, continued growth and expansion requires work on ourselves. That's why, sometimes, the hours we DON"T spend at work are important. When running your own business or in creating your own schedule, it's not easy to separate the *business-you* from the *weekend-you*. In fact, weekends may rarely exist at all on our calendar. That's okay, and it's one of the perks of running the show, as we get to dictate the terms. But life's more than business; we've got to invest in ourselves, our personal strengths, confidence and health. Mastering these things produces a strong foundation on which to rely in good times and bad. *Are you investing enough time and resources in you?*

## reflections and intentions

my thoughts and feelings on today's FLASHPOINTS include:

my intentions and action items today include:

today I am grateful for:

# If our friends tell us to "please shut up" about our ideas, we may be on the right track.

Think of the most successful people who've lived in our lifetime. No matter who comes to mind—a renowned businessperson, religious or political leader, or an international rock star (suspend judgment on whether you agree with them or not)—what they all have in common is their outreach and impact … the number of people they have affected in the world. Now, ponder the array of folks supporting this person—fans, agents, customers, stakeholders and so many more. It takes a lot of people to turn our ideas and talents into maximum world impact. That means taking every opportunity possible to talk about our ideas, in an effort to enlist and evangelize people who will support our cause. *Who will you talk to next?*

## reflections and intentions

my thoughts and feelings on today's FLASHPOINTS include:

my intentions and action items today include:

today I am grateful for:

# Burning bridges becomes irrelevant when we've built enough of them.

The old adage, "Don't burn your bridges because you'll be surprised how many times you have to cross the same river," rings true for most folks. It resonates because we rely so much on each bridge we build (old relationships) that we can't afford to burn any of them. If we have only one client in our business (one bridge) and he bullies us, we're stuck. But with multiple clients, we can give the bad ones the heave-ho. Doesn't it make more sense, then, to be in the bridge-building business, rather than in the bridge-saving business? Build bridges that will last, but if one becomes rotten, don't be afraid to blow it up. *What old bridge do you have that needs to be blown up? Should you replace it first?*

## reflections and intentions

my thoughts and feelings on today's FLASHPOINTS include:

my intentions and action items today include:

today I am grateful for:

> ## *A hard fall means a high bounce...*
> ## *if you're made of the right material.*
> ### ~ Anonymous

After five days of prompting and prodding new ideas and thoughts to come to mind, today we review what we've discovered. It's time to take a peek back at our journaling, to review our thoughts, feelings, and action items; and see how well we did. After all, self-awareness is the key to initiate growth and realize lasting change.

## weekly reflection

reflecting on my thoughts, feelings and experiences from this past week, the top three that impacted me the most include:

my top "ta-da's" (successes) from this past week include:

my top "oh-no's" (disappointments) from this past week include:

my top "ah-ha's" (discoveries) from this past week include:

## Life is like a ten speed bicycle.
## Most of us have gears we never use.

~ Charles Schulz

The end of the week is the best time to plan for the coming week. And at this point, you've reviewed the previous week and can be prepared to make changes and take actions based on thought, not re-action. You want to keep your goals in mind always. So today is your opportunity to look at yesterday's Weekly Reflection and decide what you're going to do and when. It is most often small tweaks that will lead to great success, fueled by a positive and grateful attitude.

## weekly intentions

my top "go get-'em's" (fixes) to implement this coming week include:

incomplete action items, that support my goals, to carry over into this coming week include: (schedule them now and be specific.)

new action items, that support my goals, for this coming week include: (schedule them now and be specific.)

something new I'm grateful for this week, and with whom I will share it:

# By the time you hear the thunder, it's too late to build the ark.

As we move closer to our goals, when business is booming and life is picking up steam, responsibilities can weigh us down, and a feeling of isolation can creep in. "I have obligations to keep," we lament. "Team members to support, clients to look after and services and products to provide." Suddenly, our time becomes very precious and it's difficult to keep up personal and professional appearances at public events, conferences, meetings, and mixers. Before the pendulum of success swings the other way, we must ensure we're out there spreading the word about our endeavors. The world loves hearing about success stories, and supporters can help you keep forward momentum through affirmation, encouragement and exposure. *How will you put your ventures in the public eye this week?*

## reflections and intentions

my thoughts and feelings on today's FLASHPOINTS include:

my intentions and action items today include:

today I am grateful for:

## "Right" and "control" are ugly words.

Needing to be "right" and in "control" will only get us so far. There's simply no way we'll recognize our potential with those behaviors. In fact, they'll often *discourage* progress toward our goals rather than propel our team toward them. Effective leadership means handing over the reigns to competent team members and *being okay with it!* Accept and believe that setting our personal agendas aside, opening up the floor to suggestions from our team, then mulling them over with humility, will actually grow our ideas bigger and better. All we need to do is set aside our ego, place our vision in the hands of our team, then simply facilitate ... and watch the magic happen! *What's keeping you from asking for, and truly considering, your team's opinions and ideas?*

## reflections and intentions

my thoughts and feelings on today's FLASHPOINTS include:

my intentions and action items today include:

today I am grateful for:

# Success is a journey, not a destination.

A personalized vision of what success looks like is *critically* important to reach our fullest *potential*. But don't make success the end game! It's really up to each of us to chart a course that works best for us to grow and achieve more. That discovery process is a combination of trial and error, following our gut instinct, tracking our feelings and actual results. If structure is needed with well-defined targets, we'll need to document our vision and refer back to it often for continued inspiration. If flexibility is better, just stick with something for as long as it remains fun (which is a valid vision in itself), then perhaps all the motivation and foresight required will be there already. *Are you prepared to chart your course toward your fullest potential?*

## reflections and intentions

my thoughts and feelings on today's FLASHPOINTS include:

my intentions and action items today include:

today I am grateful for:

## Give a present:
## Give your presence.

Whether at home or work, the people in our lives want and deserve more than just being in our presence ... they want to engage on a deep and meaningful level. It's particularly difficult to connect with our loved ones after a tough day at work, when our emails, struggles and strife follow us home. The key to a successful transition is to *intentionally* sign off from the office by engaging in some kind of activity that will shift our focus to what's critically important: our family and friends. A quick break between work and home to participate in a favorite sport or hobby, some meditation, or simply listening to soothing music might be the ticket for a smooth transition. *How will you disengage from work today, and present your presence?*

## reflections and intentions

my thoughts and feelings on today's FLASHPOINTS include:

my intentions and action items today include:

today I am grateful for:

# Desire without discipline will always delay your dreams.
### ~ Marcus Slaton

We've become enamored with securing a quick fix on everything, only looking for solutions that produce results *fast!* If it's not available now, we tend to move on to whatever we think can get us there the fastest. We get ourselves into trouble, however, when we substitute quickness for that much needed (and often underestimated) power of *discipline:* e.g., special quick diets and shakes to lose weight rather than the hard work of exercise and healthy eating. While *desire* is good, possessing the daily *discipline* to methodically execute on the action steps to attain long-term satisfaction, success and significance is AWESOME! *Where in your life are you seeking the quick fix rather than hunkering down and doing some plain old hard work, day in and day out?*

## reflections and intentions

my thoughts and feelings on today's FLASHPOINTS include:

my intentions and action items today include:

today I am grateful for:

> # He who deliberates fully before taking a step will spend his entire life on one leg.
>
> ~ Chinese Proverb

After five days of prompting and prodding new ideas and thoughts to come to mind, today we review what we've discovered. It's time to take a peek back at our journaling, to review our thoughts, feelings, and action items; and see how well we did. After all, self-awareness is the key to initiate growth and realize lasting change.

## weekly reflection

reflecting on my thoughts, feelings and experiences from this past week, the top three that impacted me the most include:

my top "ta-da's" (successes) from this past week include:

my top "oh-no's" (disappointments) from this past week include:

my top "ah-ha's" (discoveries) from this past week include:

> ## *Either you run the day or the day runs you.*
> ### ~ Jim Rohn

The end of the week is the best time to plan for the coming week. And at this point, you've reviewed the previous week and can be prepared to make changes and take actions based on thought, not re-action. You want to keep your goals in mind always. So today is your opportunity to look at yesterday's Weekly Reflection and decide what you're going to do and when. It is most often small tweaks that will lead to great success, fueled by a positive and grateful attitude.

## weekly intentions

my top "go get-'em's" (fixes) to implement this coming week include:

incomplete action items, that support my goals, to carry over into this coming week include: (schedule them now and be specific.)

new action items, that support my goals, for this coming week include: (schedule them now and be specific.)

something new I'm grateful for this week, and with whom I will share it:

## Life is full of ups and downs.
## You can just scream, or you can enjoy the ride.

The life of an achiever can be demanding and exhausting, yet incredibly fruitful. There are lessons to learn and experiences to endure. There are, however, no short-cuts to success; and, there are more ups and downs than a roller coaster at Magic Mountain. Wouldn't it be nice to talk to someone who's been on that ride, who can share when to brace hard, when to relax, and when the biggest plunge is coming? Get out there and build relationships with folks who've made the journey and who are bolder and brighter that you. Treat them to lunch sometime, with the possible payoff of a brain dump. Don't forget to offer to serve them in some way in return. *Who can you call who'd save you oodles of time and energy?*

## reflections and intentions

my thoughts and feelings on today's FLASHPOINTS include:

my intentions and action items today include:

today I am grateful for:

# Never surrender!
# You might give in just before the biggest achievement of your life.

As high achievers, we often take on the most demanding of tasks. At times this means feeling overwhelmed, stressed, and tired. It's enough to make us want to throw in the towel, and trade it all in for a more average life. But, hold on! Didn't you realize there'd be days like these? Yet, you chose to step into the arena, anyway. The fact is, you've always been up for the challenge … so, don't stop now. Tenacity drives us to take on opportunity after opportunity, despite the hard work and long hours required. It's disastrous to give up too early, only to miss out on a great success that's just around the corner. *What are you working on that needs a little extra "oomph" to cross the finish line?*

## reflections and intentions

my thoughts and feelings on today's FLASHPOINTS include:

my intentions and action items today include:

today I am grateful for:

# Does your team come to you with problems or solutions?

One of the most desired skills of an effective team is their ability to think of solutions before bringing problems to their leaders. Encouraging our teams to provide a solution for each problem is not only a way to increase productivity and decision-making in our organization, it can also be empowering, increasing the team's sense of ownership. Next time someone comes to us with a problem, we're to listen to their concern and then ask, "How do you think we could deal with this?" We've then started a discussion, rather than giving orders or saying, "I'll get back to you," which wastes time. More often than not, associates and colleagues have valuable ideas to contribute. *How will you foster a solutions-oriented mentality on your team?*

## reflections and intentions

my thoughts and feelings on today's FLASHPOINTS include:

my intentions and action items today include:

today I am grateful for:

# What's love got to do with it?

Well, actually, a whole lot. Do you love your life? How about your organization? How about the people you work with every day? And your family or social circle? There's no doubt that living a fulfilled life has everything to do with loving what you do and loving those around you. You might not love the menial tasks that come with achieving your goals, but there is something you can do about that. As your business and life gets busier, look to delegating, deleting or deferring non-critical tasks that don't need your involvement or input. Your time is valuable, so spend more of it doing the stuff you love and outsource the rest. Take an inventory today. *What do you love doing in your business? Do more of it.*

## reflections and intentions

my thoughts and feelings on today's FLASHPOINTS include:

my intentions and action items today include:

today I am grateful for:

## Communication 2.0

With so much of our communication and socializing happening online these days, how do we ensure our messaging is most effective? No doubt, email communications can increase efficiencies, but remember the good old days? If you wanted to speak to someone on the other side of the office, you got up and walked there. Set the standard for others to emulate—talk to people face-to-face when it's important, and encourage your team to do the same. Why? Well, have you noticed that sometimes emailing works against you by poorly relaying tone and slowing down the communication process? More face-to-face talks and actual phone calls could help teammates, family members, and clients build a relationship with you, instead of their computer monitors. *How effectively do you communicate?*

### reflections and intentions

my thoughts and feelings on today's FLASHPOINTS include:

my intentions and action items today include:

today I am grateful for:

> # People see the world not as it is,
> ## but as they are.
>
> ### ~ Al Lee

After five days of prompting and prodding new ideas and thoughts to come to mind, today we review what we've discovered. It's time to take a peek back at our journaling, to review our thoughts, feelings, and action items; and see how well we did. After all, self-awareness is the key to initiate growth and realize lasting change.

## weekly reflection

reflecting on my thoughts, feelings and experiences from this past week, the top three that impacted me the most include:

my top "ta-da's" (successes) from this past week include:

my top "oh-no's" (disappointments) from this past week include:

my top "ah-ha's" (discoveries) from this past week include:

> ## The greatest motivational act one person can do for another is to listen.
> ### ~ Roy E. Moody

The end of the week is the best time to plan for the coming week. And at this point, you've reviewed the previous week and can be prepared to make changes and take actions based on thought, not re-action. You want to keep your goals in mind always. So today is your opportunity to look at yesterday's Weekly Reflection and decide what you're going to do and when. It is most often small tweaks that will lead to great success, fueled by a positive and grateful attitude.

## weekly intentions

my top "go get-'em's" (fixes) to implement this coming week include:

incomplete action items, that support my goals, to carry over into this coming week include: (schedule them now and be specific.)

new action items, that support my goals, for this coming week include: (schedule them now and be specific.)

something new I'm grateful for this week, and with whom I will share it:

## A closed mind and heart keeps many things out, including new ideas.

It's really amazing that the moment we pry ourselves open to the possibility of a new idea or approach, it manifests and presents itself to us! We've all experienced times when we start thinking about something new or an unsolved problem and suddenly iterations of ideas and solutions begin to appear around us for the next few days. Is it Law of Attraction, social trends, or the Reticular Activating System in our brains? Who cares? It's *awesome* to experience! Just remember that whenever we need a fresh perspective, inspiration, or solution, the answers are already around us ... we just need to be open to learning them. In our heads *and* our hearts. *What messages and conversations are going on around you that you can tune into?*

### reflections and intentions

my thoughts and feelings on today's FLASHPOINTS include:

my intentions and action items today include:

today I am grateful for:

# Being true to our word makes leadership a whole lot easier.

Making daily decisions is challenging for many and forces some into a severe case of analysis-paralysis, preventing them from taking action. Those gray areas of life can be difficult to negotiate, as there may not be a clear right or wrong, winner or loser. But, if at the very core of all our actions is being true to ourselves, our values and our goals, and acting in the best interest of those involved with our ventures, suddenly putting ourselves out there isn't as challenging as we imagined. If we only take actions consistent with our values, even if the results are less than expected, at least we haven't compromised who we are. *How have you made speaking the truth on a daily basis part of who you are?*

## reflections and intentions

my thoughts and feelings on today's FLASHPOINTS include:

my intentions and action items today include:

today I am grateful for:

## If you don't have time to do it right, when will you have time to do it over?

~ John Wooden

Emergencies and crises aside, before making that phone call to our mentors or trusted advisors, let's show we're serious about our goals by doing some real planning. Effective planning helps crystallize what's known and unknown and lays out in gory detail what we anticipate will happen. Our extra efforts offer our mentors the chance to red-line our plan for crystal clarity and inspires them to want to offer more guidance. Proper planning also prepares us to ask profound questions and offers the emotional freedom to effectively listen. Time is a precious resource, so we must seek a healthy balance between doing things right the first time and avoiding analysis paralysis in pursuit of perfection. *What plans do you need to complete before presenting them to your mentor or coach?*

## reflections and intentions

my thoughts and feelings on today's FLASHPOINTS include:

my intentions and action items today include:

today I am grateful for:

# Wow, that's SLEEK!

Streamlined. Efficient. Classy. Top of the line. Yesterday's style meets today's chic. Precise handling, with sporty controls and state-of-the-art features. Smooth sailing on the open roads; unbreakable in rough terrain. Effortless cruise controls for long journeys; zero to one hundred when we need it. Satisfaction guaranteed, with a lifetime warranty. Sure, it sounds we're talking about a car, but why shouldn't it also describe our professional endeavors and personal development goals? *How can you rev up the sleek factor today in whatever you're doing?*

## reflections and intentions

my thoughts and feelings on today's FLASHPOINTS include:

my intentions and action items today include:

today I am grateful for:

# Very freaky!

Many entrepreneurs start as a one-person show, personally responsible for everything in their new venture. It's no wonder that, years down the track, they feel trapped still working on the intricacies of the business rather than improving its general direction. Handing over some decision making and outsourcing tasks, such as bookkeeping and payroll, could be the answer to freedom's call. Reality check: being control freaks is stunting the growth of our businesses! Forget that we might know how to do these tasks better than anyone else—doing everything yourself is not sustainable! Make a list of tasks worked on frequently and then ask, "What do I hate doing and wish I could spend less time on?" Next, delegate away! *What are you planning to delegate tomorrow?*

## reflections and intentions

my thoughts and feelings on today's FLASHPOINTS include:

my intentions and action items today include:

today I am grateful for:

> ## Life isn't measured by the number of breaths we take, but by the moments that take our breath away.
>
> ### ~ Anonymous

After five days of prompting and prodding new ideas and thoughts to come to mind, today we review what we've discovered. It's time to take a peek back at our journaling, to review our thoughts, feelings, and action items; and see how well we did. After all, self-awareness is the key to initiate growth and realize lasting change.

## weekly reflection

reflecting on my thoughts, feelings and experiences from this past week, the top three that impacted me the most include:

my top "ta-da's" (successes) from this past week include:

my top "oh-no's" (disappointments) from this past week include:

my top "ah-ha's" (discoveries) from this past week include:

> ## *Obstacles are those frightful things you see when you take your eyes off your goal.*
> ~ Henry Ford

The end of the week is the best time to plan for the coming week. And at this point, you've reviewed the previous week and can be prepared to make changes and take actions based on thought, not re-action. You want to keep your goals in mind always. So today is your opportunity to look at yesterday's Weekly Reflection and decide what you're going to do and when. It is most often small tweaks that will lead to great success, fueled by a positive and grateful attitude.

## weekly intentions

my top "go get-'em's" (fixes) to implement this coming week include:

incomplete action items, that support my goals, to carry over into this coming week include: (schedule them now and be specific.)

new action items, that support my goals, for this coming week include: (schedule them now and be specific.)

something new I'm grateful for this week, and with whom I will share it:

## Success comes from taking action... over and over again.

Having a great idea is a great start, but that's all it is ... an idea. Unless we're constantly taking action on those ideas, they don't have much value other than being a pleasant little dream. At the very basis of our success is our ability to transform ideas into actions to be taken by us and others who believe in our cause. So, if we want to change the world, make an impact in our communities and achieve success, we must take that first small step, and then take another. Our continued success depends on taking small actions consistent with achieving our goals over and over again. *What action will you take today to move your ideas one step closer to reality?*

## reflections and intentions

my thoughts and feelings on today's FLASHPOINTS include:

my intentions and action items today include:

today I am grateful for:

# Where do opportunities come from? Achievers create opportunities where others see work.

When it comes to opportunity, it's rarely just a matter of good fortune. Not often can we say it was simply meant to be. And only sometimes can we attribute it to being in the right place at the right time. Most of the time, opportunity comes from serving others first, generating good word-of-mouth, expanding our sphere of influence, creating our own opportunities from nothing, and working hard to achieve excellence in every piece of work we put our name to. Building on our credibility, serving others, and demonstrating results will get us there. *Where will your next opportunity come from?*

## reflections and intentions

my thoughts and feelings on today's FLASHPOINTS include:

my intentions and action items today include:

today I am grateful for:

## We must stumble in the dark before the light of passion illuminates our vision.

There are myriad conversations going on around us about vision and passion. It can feel nightmarish for those whose light bulbs haven't yet been lit. The truth is, it takes work to discover where to plug in. Only a very lucky few knew from kindergarten what they wanted to do. But how are we, the less lucky, supposed to find "it?" Step 1: Stop waiting … while a great idea might hit us out of the blue, they'll normally hit while we're DOING something. Step 2: If something sounds interesting, dive in and see where it leads—a natural talent or affinity may appear. Eventually, the light bulb will flicker and then start to glow brightly. *Is your passion burning bright enough to light your path? Now what?*

## reflections and intentions

my thoughts and feelings on today's FLASHPOINTS include:

my intentions and action items today include:

today I am grateful for:

## Be bold.
## Be courageous,
## Live a more fulfilled life.

If you've been blessed to see courage in action, you've recognized that the lives of the courageous are punctuated with greatness, and they possess an air of confidence that's intoxicating. Of the mother who, to free her trapped child, lifts her vehicle (while in the absence of fear she could barely budge its weight); or when the meek finally throw off the chains of his aggressor, do we call them weak? Pull back the curtain and we'll recognize that it's courage that provides the wisdom to be humble and sustains us on our journey toward our dreams. We may not always be right and we may not always win, but we have the chance to try again tomorrow. *Where are you able to dig deep, be bold, and try again?*

## reflections and intentions

my thoughts and feelings on today's FLASHPOINTS include:

my intentions and action items today include:

today I am grateful for:

## Accountability: it only works when we want it to.

Being the boss is tough, regardless of our position within the organizational pyramid. It takes tenacity, capabilities that cover myriad tasks, and the confidence to push through barriers. Even if we think we're at the top, we're not—we still must answer to the customer or investor. So if we think accountability is for "others," or only for us to dish out, THINK AGAIN! Ultimately, we answer to our customers—internal or external. Answering consistently and on-time requires discipline; to forge that into a habit, we've got to dare to be accountable to someone other than ourselves. Finding a coach or someone who will be just as invested in our efforts as we are is the key. *To whom do you answer, and to whom are you accountable?*

## reflections and intentions

my thoughts and feelings on today's FLASHPOINTS include:

my intentions and action items today include:

today I am grateful for:

> ## *Start by doing what's necessary; then do what's possible; and suddenly you are doing the impossible.*
>
> ### ~ St. Francis of Assisi

After five days of prompting and prodding new ideas and thoughts to come to mind, today we review what we've discovered. It's time to take a peek back at our journaling, to review our thoughts, feelings, and action items; and see how well we did. After all, self-awareness is the key to initiate growth and realize lasting change.

## weekly reflection

reflecting on my thoughts, feelings and experiences from this past week, the top three that impacted me the most include:

my top "ta-da's" (successes) from this past week include:

my top "oh-no's" (disappointments) from this past week include:

my top "ah-ha's" (discoveries) from this past week include:

> # One thing about the school of experience is that it will repeat the lesson if you flunk the first time.
> ### ~ Anonymous

The end of the week is the best time to plan for the coming week. And at this point, you've reviewed the previous week and can be prepared to make changes and take actions based on thought, not re-action. You want to keep your goals in mind always. So today is your opportunity to look at yesterday's Weekly Reflection and decide what you're going to do and when. It is most often small tweaks that will lead to great success, fueled by a positive and grateful attitude.

## weekly intentions

my top "go get-'em's" (fixes) to implement this coming week include:

incomplete action items, that support my goals, to carry over into this coming week include: (schedule them now and be specific.)

new action items, that support my goals, for this coming week include: (schedule them now and be specific.)

something new I'm grateful for this week, and with whom I will share it:

> # I've heard a positive attitude can over-come anything. I'm not sure about that, but I am sure that a positive attitude attracts other positive people.

As leaders and achievers, life has extreme ups and downs, and it can be challenging to maintain a positive attitude at all times. But look at it this way: Have you ever desperately wanted to work or collaborate with someone who doesn't exude positivity when they talk about their projects? I didn't think so! Our goals, vision and projects rely on our positive attitude to attract other like-minded, positive people. Now that's something to smile about! *Where in your life can you boost your positivity?*

## reflections and intentions

my thoughts and feelings on today's FLASHPOINTS include:

my intentions and action items today include:

today I am grateful for:

# Create a routine to maximize productivity.

Sometimes, no matter how organized we are, too much of our day is spent answering questions. Rather than getting through our own to-do list, we spend a disproportionate time with our team, helping them move forward with their own workloads. It's times like these that having a daily or weekly routine can boost productivity. For example, meeting with the team each morning for a short block of time (in the hotel/restaurant industry this is called a "line up") will cut down our time answering questions throughout the day. Also, marking out blocks of time during the week for undisturbed work, encouraging the team to do the same, works wonders. *What would be the effect in productivity and morale if you tried one or both of these?*

## reflections and intentions

my thoughts and feelings on today's FLASHPOINTS include:

my intentions and action items today include:

today I am grateful for:

## Don't give up.
## Ever!
## The world depends on it.

Being a leader responsible for change and innovation has its challenges: budgets, deadlines, Gantt charts, performance reviews, productivity, team morale, etc. But let's not forget the unlimited rewards that are possible: the most noteworthy are leaving our fingerprint and legacy on the world, contributing to progress and, of course, living out our personal dreams and desires. What would happen if world leaders and business innovators suddenly gave up on their aspirations one by one? The negative effects would be massive and too numerous to put into words here. Next time you get stuck finding a way to move forward, ask yourself: *Does the world, and my sphere of influence, really depend on my ideas, efforts, and energy to move forward?* The answer is, *Yes!* Now, go take action.

## reflections and intentions

my thoughts and feelings on today's FLASHPOINTS include:

my intentions and action items today include:

today I am grateful for:

# Letting go isn't the end of the world; it's the beginning of a new life.

Some leaders are self-confessed control freaks. Others are in denial. Some crave the limelight, while others prefer anonymity. Which category best suits you? It's okay to be in any one of the categories (or none at all), as long as you're aware of your strengths and can rally the appropriate resources as needed. At times, we must maintain a tight hold on the reins of our organizations and be involved in every decision and step. Other times—actually, most of the time—it's best to take the back seat and let your team call the shots and feel empowered, while you offer guidance and simply give them the glory of their accomplishments. *What area of your life or business needs the fresh breeze of a new beginning?*

## reflections and intentions

my thoughts and feelings on today's FLASHPOINTS include:

my intentions and action items today include:

today I am grateful for:

## Listen up:
## Stop listening! Start learning!

Given our "information is everywhere" culture, sensory overload is bound to happen. It's not a question of if or when, but how we'll handle it. While information gathering may offer fun educational opportunities, it can lead us down a rabbit hole, distracting us from our calling. When our vision becomes murky, or when doubts begin to surface, it's time to scale back the number and frequency of information inputs. It's time to stop listening (perhaps that means a break from the seminar circuit or even the daily news) and start the *real* learning, by taking action and applying the information we've received. *What information have you gathered (like a seminar how-to manual) that, if applied, would add significant value to your plan or get you closer to your goal?*

## reflections and intentions

my thoughts and feelings on today's FLASHPOINTS include:

my intentions and action items today include:

today I am grateful for:

> ## We learn more by looking for the answer to a question and not finding it than we do from learning the answer itself.
>
> ### ~ Lloyd Alexander

After five days of prompting and prodding new ideas and thoughts to come to mind, today we review what we've discovered. It's time to take a peek back at our journaling, to review our thoughts, feelings, and action items; and see how well we did. After all, self-awareness is the key to initiate growth and realize lasting change.

## weekly reflection

reflecting on my thoughts, feelings and experiences from this past week, the top three that impacted me the most include:

my top "ta-da's" (successes) from this past week include:

my top "oh-no's" (disappointments) from this past week include:

my top "ah-ha's" (discoveries) from this past week include:

> *In prosperity our friends know us;*
> *in adversity we know our friends.*
> ~ John Churton Collins

The end of the week is the best time to plan for the coming week. And at this point, you've reviewed the previous week and can be prepared to make changes and take actions based on thought, not re-action. You want to keep your goals in mind always. So today is your opportunity to look at yesterday's Weekly Reflection and decide what you're going to do and when. It is most often small tweaks that will lead to great success, fueled by a positive and grateful attitude.

## weekly intentions

my top "go get-'em's" (fixes) to implement this coming week include:

incomplete action items, that support my goals, to carry over into this coming week include: (schedule them now and be specific.)

new action items, that support my goals, for this coming week include: (schedule them now and be specific.)

something new I'm grateful for this week, and with whom I will share it:

## Business is a world of trial and error, where failures lead to success.

The determination to push on through failures is one indicator of a true achiever. The person succeeding in business without maneuvering through any roadblocks is indeed a rare exception. The business world is more competitive, dynamic, and inventive these days than ever, so entrepreneurs and business leaders are required to take risks, forge ahead where no other business has gone before, and constantly put their ideas out there to be critiqued. That means facing failure from time to time. But more importantly, it means learning from our trials and daring to undertake them all over again ... as opposed to assuming the fetal position and feeling sorry for ourselves. *What lessons have you learned from your most recent failure? Have you written them down anywhere so you don't repeat them?*

### reflections and intentions

my thoughts and feelings on today's FLASHPOINTS include:

my intentions and action items today include:

today I am grateful for:

# Sometimes we need to cut our hair to find the true color.

We often rely on the reflection of a mirror to assess our physical appearance. But isn't the reflection only as good as the mirror? Partially. In reality, it's based mostly on our own PERCEPTION of ourselves. For example, someone who's anorexic sees fat where none exists. This truth is not limited to our physical being, but to all areas of our self-perception. Think professionally, relationally, spiritually … or wherever we're seeking excellence. Our perception may be totally off the mark, and that's when we need to throw out the mirror and stop lying to ourselves. Often only mentors and loved ones can truly reflect reality to us. *Who are you using to reflect your true image? Are they bold enough to share the truth? Are you courageous enough to listen?*

## reflections and intentions

my thoughts and feelings on today's FLASHPOINTS include:

my intentions and action items today include:

today I am grateful for:

# Be, be, be prepared ...
## to serve and assist your network.

The very best networking events are especially powerful when *everyone* benefits. Too often, networking is confused with *taking*. To create effective networking opportunities, we must create fruitful relationships ... so, we must be prepared to serve others. Otherwise, our first impression at that next networking event on our calendar could be a flop. Before attending a meeting, event or launch, think about what the objective is in attending. We need to ask ourselves, "What kind of relationships am I prepared to build? Rather than just collecting business cards, how can I truly serve these folks?" Being specific with ourselves can help us identify the key details or values we should mention when describing our business to new people. *How can you better SERVE those who join your network?*

## reflections and intentions

my thoughts and feelings on today's FLASHPOINTS include:

my intentions and action items today include:

today I am grateful for:

# What's *really* on your mind?

It's no secret that the workplace can be a breeding ground for hearsay, unnecessary gossip, and whispers behind closed doors. What may at first seem harmless could quickly erode trust and morale. Left unchecked, it becomes destructive and even dangerous. Often, those who employ a more direct communication style, who waste no time playing polite, are accused of being too open, too honest and even disrespectful. How do we get the balance of communication among our team just right? First, talk to people, not *about* them, even if discussing work performance— involve them, so it's constructive. Second, it's the old adage of practicing what you preach: if you don't like gossip, don't participate. The balance of direct and respectful communication wins the day. *What communication habits are floating about your workspace?*

## reflections and intentions

my thoughts and feelings on today's FLASHPOINTS include:

my intentions and action items today include:

today I am grateful for:

# Risk nothing, gain nothing, be nothing.

Although the word "risk" is often used with negative connotations, calculated risk-taking often leads to uncharted success. Why is it, then, that many of us avoid moving forward when risk is involved? In a word, fear. Those who find risk particularly challenging (even debilitating) are usually focusing on what they could lose, rather than on the gain they may realize on the other side of fear. Reflect on your early childhood and you'll recognize that some of your most joyous moments came from taking risks. So share your success plan with a trusted advisor, take action, and move out. Expect to stumble once in a while, but remember that success is 99% failure, and just keep moving forward. *What calculated risks could move you closer to your potential?*

## reflections and intentions

my thoughts and feelings on today's FLASHPOINTS include:

my intentions and action items today include:

today I am grateful for:

> ## Time invested in improving ourselves cuts down on time wasted in disapproving of others.
>
> ~ **Anonymous**

After five days of prompting and prodding new ideas and thoughts to come to mind, today we review what we've discovered. It's time to take a peek back at our journaling, to review our thoughts, feelings, and action items; and see how well we did. After all, self-awareness is the key to initiate growth and realize lasting change.

## weekly reflection

reflecting on my thoughts, feelings and experiences from this past week, the top three that impacted me the most include:

my top "ta-da's" (successes) from this past week include:

my top "oh-no's" (disappointments) from this past week include:

my top "ah-ha's" (discoveries) from this past week include:

> ## *Successful people are always looking for opportunities to help others. Unsuccessful people are always asking, 'What's in it for me?'*
>
> ### ~ Brian Tracy

The end of the week is the best time to plan for the coming week. And at this point, you've reviewed the previous week and can be prepared to make changes and take actions based on thought, not re-action. You want to keep your goals in mind always. So today is your opportunity to look at yesterday's Weekly Reflection and decide what you're going to do and when. It is most often small tweaks that will lead to great success, fueled by a positive and grateful attitude.

## weekly intentions

my top "go get-'em's" (fixes) to implement this coming week include:

incomplete action items, that support my goals, to carry over into this coming week include: (schedule them now and be specific.)

new action items, that support my goals, for this coming week include: (schedule them now and be specific.)

something new I'm grateful for this week, and with whom I will share it:

# Sticks and stones may break my bones, but words can heal my heart.

Have you ever had one of those days where little seemed to be going right, but then someone said something kind, understanding or complimentary? It's hard to stay in a slump when that happens. Words are powerful! Just like negative words can cut deeply, positive comments have the power to heal and create confidence, success and happiness in others. Isn't that amazing? Suffice it to say, we shouldn't hold back from telling people when we're proud, satisfied, or just plain happy to have them in our lives. After all, who knows what kind of slump you could help pull someone out of with just a few words? *What healing words can you speak into someone's life today?*

## reflections and intentions

my thoughts and feelings on today's FLASHPOINTS include:

my intentions and action items today include:

today I am grateful for:

## Which came first,
## the opportunity or the success?

It seems that recognized leaders and established businesses generate bigger and brighter opportunities simply because they've become well known. The fact is, it takes years (or even a lifetime) to create enduring success in any field. We must open our minds, keep a watchful eye, and *create* an occasion to bring value to those around us ... then opportunity will find us. We must stop focusing on the timing of that big break and worrying about whether it will come complete with a neon sign pointing toward success. Every interaction and every connection is a critical step on our path to significance. Don't miss any critical steps on that path by passively waiting for opportunity to come knocking! *What opportunity will you create to serve others today?*

## reflections and intentions

my thoughts and feelings on today's FLASHPOINTS include:

my intentions and action items today include:

today I am grateful for:

# What's love got to do with it?

Well actually, a whole lot. Do you love your life? How about your organization? How about the people you work with every day? And your family or social circle? There's no doubt that living a fulfilled life is directly connected to how well we're loving what we do and loving those around us. We may not love the menial tasks that come along with achieving our goals, but there is something we can do about that. As your business and life gets busier, consider delegating, deleting and deferring tasks and projects. Your time is valuable, so spend more of it doing the stuff you love and outsource the rest. Take an inventory today. *What do you love doing that supports your mission?*

## reflections and intentions

my thoughts and feelings on today's FLASHPOINTS include:

my intentions and action items today include:

today I am grateful for:

> # Don't let yourself go
> # 'Cause everybody cries
> # And everybody hurts sometimes
>
> ~ R.E.M., Everybody Hurts

Don't we all love an open, honest conversation? One where we can say what's really on our minds? But it takes backbone to let the ego get pummeled for a time when we ask for feedback. That conversation, when delivered with tough love, can be the most rewarding one of our lives. The truth can hurt, and it takes a big person to receive it with humility, give it due consideration, and follow up with action. Of course, we shouldn't allow just anyone to do this—it must be someone who really "gets" us, who understands both our plight and our plans. Find a candid, forthright mentor, and you'll have this depth of relationship. *How well does your mentor speak truth into your life? What question do you wish they'd ask?*

## reflections and intentions

my thoughts and feelings on today's FLASHPOINTS include:

my intentions and action items today include:

today I am grateful for:

# The most powerful antidote to stress is choosing one thought over another.

Some say stress is healthy: working under pressure is how we get things done! Others say stress is … well, stressful. No matter our take on stress, we all experience its different forms, and we all have our limits. What's most important is recognizing when we're experiencing healthy and unhealthy stresses in our lives and then responding accordingly by associating the appropriate thoughts to our current situation. Despite its often negative stigma, with the proper mindset, stress can work in our favor. The key for many people is harnessing that on-edge feeling and thinking positively when experiencing busy times. For example, consider a looming deadline as an opportunity to complete a task successfully and cross it off the to-do list. *How will you get stress on your side this week?*

## reflections and intentions

my thoughts and feelings on today's FLASHPOINTS include:

my intentions and action items today include:

today I am grateful for:

> ## It is the nature of man to rise to greatness if greatness is expected of him.
>
> ### ~ John Steinbeck

After five days of prompting and prodding new ideas and thoughts to come to mind, today we review what we've discovered. It's time to take a peek back at our journaling, to review our thoughts, feelings, and action items; and see how well we did. After all, self-awareness is the key to initiate growth and realize lasting change.

## weekly reflection

reflecting on my thoughts, feelings and experiences from this past week, the top three that impacted me the most include:

my top "ta-da's" (successes) from this past week include:

my top "oh-no's" (disappointments) from this past week include:

my top "ah-ha's" (discoveries) from this past week include:

> ## *If you can dream it, you can do it. Always remember this whole thing was started by a mouse.*
>
> ### ~ Walt Disney

The end of the week is the best time to plan for the coming week. And at this point, you've reviewed the previous week and can be prepared to make changes and take actions based on thought, not re-action. You want to keep your goals in mind always. So today is your opportunity to look at yesterday's Weekly Reflection and decide what you're going to do and when. It is most often small tweaks that will lead to great success, fueled by a positive and grateful attitude.

## weekly intentions

my top "go get-'em's" (fixes) to implement this coming week include:

incomplete action items, that support my goals, to carry over into this coming week include: (schedule them now and be specific.)

new action items, that support my goals, for this coming week include: (schedule them now and be specific.)

something new I'm grateful for this week, and with whom I will share it:

FLASHPOINTS for achievers

# Customer Service is not a department ... it's an ATTITUDE!

My biggest gripe about the business world is experiencing poor customer service. I just can't stand it, and none of us should have to. Maybe that's why it hurts my heart so much when we fall short in my organizations. I can't help thinking this has something to do with people not being happy, not caring enough for the client, or simply being overwhelmed. Have you ever witnessed this in your own organization? And how do you deal with it? Consider this when hiring candidates: attitude is more important than experience. How about this? For those folks who aren't cutting it, cut them loose; and to reinforce positive behaviors, reward those folks who are exceeding service expectations. *What evidence do you have that your organization is providing exceptional customer service?*

## reflections and intentions

my thoughts and feelings on today's FLASHPOINTS include:

my intentions and action items today include:

today I am grateful for:

# Both greatness and mediocrity are self-imposed. Choose wisely.

There's only so long that high achievers can play the safe hand and blend into the ashen background of mediocrity. At some point we need to step out on the ledge and leap into the unknown. Sounds scary, right? But what if we drove through that fear? It could just give our current circumstance a fighting chance at exciting and uncharted success ... or it could help us break through the plateaus in our careers, relationships and lives. If the results aren't met with immediate success, we'll learn a whole lot about how to approach our next risk with more skill and confidence. So, no matter the outcome, we'll achieve significant success after all. *In what areas of life have you settled for mediocrity, when you ought to be striving for greatness?*

## reflections and intentions

my thoughts and feelings on today's FLASHPOINTS include:

my intentions and action items today include:

today I am grateful for:

## Never can say goodbye...
## No, No, No, No ...

At some point in life, we've all come across those golden team members, partners or stakeholders on whom we've relied to assist with our growth, maturation, or healing process. Over time, though, for whatever reason, we've parted ways and said "goodbye"—despite the integral role they've played in helping us achieve our goals. How often do we revisit these relationships? As our careers and businesses grow, it may prove beneficial to stay in touch with these folks ... who knows when they may become part of our valuable extended family once more? And besides, wouldn't it be great to have them out there sharing positive stories about working with us? *What one person will you reconnect with this week?*

## reflections and intentions

my thoughts and feelings on today's FLASHPOINTS include:

my intentions and action items today include:

today I am grateful for:

# Competition becomes insignificant when YOU are the brand.

The more we achieve, the more prone we become to copycats and competition, the more critical it becomes that our online profiles, branding and marketing messages accurately speak for us. Of course, face-to-face interactions are still mission-critical to learn how to effectively serve our constituents; but sadly, it's not always practical to maintain the personal touch when moving at breakneck speed, or once we've grown our organization to an empire. When our brand is authentic and our marketing material is top-notch, it's much easier for fans, followers, customers and clients to serve and support our efforts through viral buzz and positive word of mouth ... and it's much more difficult for the competition to copy our efforts. *Does every element of your brand and messaging reflect the authentic you?*

## reflections and intentions

my thoughts and feelings on today's FLASHPOINTS include:

my intentions and action items today include:

today I am grateful for:

## A great man once said ... something inspirational.

So many powerful stories and speeches start with quotes... and they really do motivate and inspire. But how often do we set the tone of our endeavors by capturing our own words and stories to share with people? Sure, we can look to other leaders and trailblazers for inspiration, but we also ought to look to (or create) our own mission and vision statements to capture the meaning of our personal North Star and use that to guide our efforts. We should be able to express, in just one sentence, the big vision of our business or project ... to create one powerful, truthful sentence that will inform and inspire our entire sphere of influence to take action toward our goal. *What wise words will people quote you on?*

## reflections and intentions

my thoughts and feelings on today's FLASHPOINTS include:

my intentions and action items today include:

today I am grateful for:

> **If you aren't fired with enthusiasm,
> you will be fired with enthusiasm.**
>
> ~ Vince Lombardi

After five days of prompting and prodding new ideas and thoughts to come to mind, today we review what we've discovered. It's time to take a peek back at our journaling, to review our thoughts, feelings, and action items; and see how well we did. After all, self-awareness is the key to initiate growth and realize lasting change.

## weekly reflection

reflecting on my thoughts, feelings and experiences from this past week, the top three that impacted me the most include:

my top "ta-da's" (successes) from this past week include:

my top "oh-no's" (disappointments) from this past week include:

my top "ah-ha's" (discoveries) from this past week include:

> ## In the absence of clearly-defined goals, we become strangely loyal to performing daily trivia until ultimately we become enslaved by it.
> ### ~ Robert Heinlein

The end of the week is the best time to plan for the coming week. And at this point, you've reviewed the previous week and can be prepared to make changes and take actions based on thought, not re-action. You want to keep your goals in mind always. So today is your opportunity to look at yesterday's Weekly Reflection and decide what you're going to do and when. It is most often small tweaks that will lead to great success, fueled by a positive and grateful attitude.

## weekly intentions

my top "go get-'em's" (fixes) to implement this coming week include:

incomplete action items, that support my goals, to carry over into this coming week include: (schedule them now and be specific.)

new action items, that support my goals, for this coming week include: (schedule them now and be specific.)

something new I'm grateful for this week, and with whom I will share it:

# Push through fear to reach the other side.

Overcoming obstacles is a lifelong activity for true leaders and achievers. Fear can be the biggest hurdle keeping us from achieving our fullest potential and living a life of significance. But it's scary out there, and we're all afraid of something, right? And isn't it safer on *this* side of the obstacle? Okay, STOP! Don't use "safe" as an excuse not to push through fear. Take a deep breath, close your eyes and catch a glimpse of the good life that's just on the other side of the obstacle. Focus on life after the fear; life where we can achieve everything we want, where we can be ourselves, free from the paralyzing influence of fear. Are you ready? Kick that barrier down! *What do you see on the other side?*

## reflections and intentions

my thoughts and feelings on today's FLASHPOINTS include:

my intentions and action items today include:

today I am grateful for:

> ## Loyalty begets courage.
> ## Courage begets sacrifice.
> ## Sacrifice begets love.
> ## Love begets loyalty.

It's likely we've built up quite a rapport with those key people in our organization (and life) who have been around since the early days. They tend to sacrifice on our behalf, stand arm-in-arm with us when facing challenges, and become reliable leaders, advisors, and confidants. But, could the environment and relationship be getting a little stale for them? If we don't afford these people our trust, offer them our love, and provide the freedom and resources to improve their station, systems and performance, how will we ever fully honor and respect them? We must make it a priority to engage with long-term loyalists to make sure they aren't getting stale. *What do you need to do to revitalize your loyalists?*

## reflections and intentions

my thoughts and feelings on today's FLASHPOINTS include:

my intentions and action items today include:

today I am grateful for:

# Teamwork is the fuel that allows common people to attain uncommon results.

When it comes to opportunity, it's rarely just a matter of good fortune. Not often can we say it was simply meant to be. And only on occasion can we attribute it to being in the right place at the right time. Usually, opportunity comes from serving others first, generating positive word-of-mouth, expanding our spheres of influence, creating our own opportunities from nothing and working hard to achieve excellence in every piece of work on which we put our name. Building on our credibility, serving others and demonstrating results will get us there. *Where will your next opportunity come from?*

## reflections and intentions

my thoughts and feelings on today's FLASHPOINTS include:

my intentions and action items today include:

today I am grateful for:

## To do or don't.
## That is the question.

The best "to-do" list doesn't have actions on it for very long because, ideally, we set goals and get each task done, making way for new action items. That love/hate relationship we often have with our to-do list has a lot to do with our own procrastination. If that sounds familiar, it's time to clean it up! If you have difficulty getting pressing tasks completed, be honest with yourself about why. The fact is, when we avoid completing important tasks and tell ourselves "it's not the best use of my time," it's probably because the task is outside our area of strength, or we're simply not passionate about it. Next time, move those kinds of items to your "to-don't" list. *What to-do items can you delete, defer or delegate?*

## reflections and intentions

my thoughts and feelings on today's FLASHPOINTS include:

my intentions and action items today include:

today I am grateful for:

# For an unbiased view of how we value ourselves, take inventory of the people surrounding us.

The people we spend the most time with will have either a positive or a negative impact on our projects, businesses, and relationships. Knowing this, if we truly aspire to achieve great things, shouldn't we surround ourselves with great people who have traveled the path before us? Sure, there are times when we need to be the mentor, pouring ourselves into others around us; but that can't be the bulk of our time. The fastest way to shorten our learning curve, expand our capacity, increase our sphere of influence, and move toward significance, is to surround ourselves with those who see greatness in us. It may sound harsh, but it's time to take inventory of our friends and influencers. *Who are your most significant daily influencers? Why?*

## reflections and intentions

my thoughts and feelings on today's FLASHPOINTS include:

my intentions and action items today include:

today I am grateful for:

> ## *The best angle from which to approach a problem is the Try-angle.*
> ### ~ Anonymous

After five days of prompting and prodding new ideas and thoughts to come to mind, today we review what we've discovered. It's time to take a peek back at our journaling, to review our thoughts, feelings, and action items; and see how well we did. After all, self-awareness is the key to initiate growth and realize lasting change.

## weekly reflection

reflecting on my thoughts, feelings and experiences from this past week, the top three that impacted me the most include:

my top "ta-da's" (successes) from this past week include:

my top "oh-no's" (disappointments) from this past week include:

my top "ah-ha's" (discoveries) from this past week include:

> **Live not in yesterdays, Look back and you may sorrow. Live precisely for today, Look forward to tomorrow.**
>
> ~ J.J. Hulsgen

The end of the week is the best time to plan for the coming week. And at this point, you've reviewed the previous week and can be prepared to make changes and take actions based on thought, not re-action. You want to keep your goals in mind always. So today is your opportunity to look at yesterday's Weekly Reflection and decide what you're going to do and when. It is most often small tweaks that will lead to great success, fueled by a positive and grateful attitude.

## weekly intentions

my top "go get-'em's" (fixes) to implement this coming week include:

incomplete action items, that support my goals, to carry over into this coming week include: (schedule them now and be specific.)

new action items, that support my goals, for this coming week include: (schedule them now and be specific.)

something new I'm grateful for this week, and with whom I will share it:

# I need time off from my own bad behavior.

As leaders, we set the standards of excellence for our organizations, accepting the duty to provide, protect and nurture our teams. When was your last reality check on whether you're actually walking your own talk regarding these key responsibilities? Take a deep breath and reflect on the expectations you have of others. Now, reflect on your own behaviors. Do you keep people waiting, miss important deadlines, fail to fulfill promises, breach your own integrity standards, or show bad sportsmanship? Reality bites, doesn't it? Yes, you're the leader. Sure, you may work harder and longer. Heck no, you're not exempt from your own Code of Conduct nor the behaviors you expect from your own teammates. *How will you ensure your own actions meet the standards you expect of others?*

## reflections and intentions

my thoughts and feelings on today's FLASHPOINTS include:

my intentions and action items today include:

today I am grateful for:

# Leadership is a choice.
# Are you in, or are you out?

What may start out as us taking on an early leadership role to avoid the mundane, 9-to-5 job of achieving someone else's dreams can sometimes lead to questioning who we are and why we're working so hard! Aren't "leadership" roles supposed to be easier than "worker" roles? Hell, no! Real leaders share the burden with their team when it gets too heavy, keeping their team focused by ensuring they are properly prepared to handle the heat, stress and unfair realities of everyday life. We step into the leadership gap because we want to make a positive difference. Leadership comes with the high price of determination, dedication and responsibility. *If you can't stand the heat, get out of the kitchen! Are you going to step up, or should you step out?*

## reflections and intentions

my thoughts and feelings on today's FLASHPOINTS include:

my intentions and action items today include:

today I am grateful for:

## Manipulation is cheating, not leading.

Receiving praise, expanding our influence, and winning friends and allies is much simpler than it seems. None of us needs a weekend workshop or bestselling book on manipulation to find out how. Here's how hard work, integrity, and authenticity are all it takes to make lasting friends in business and life. A strategic mind, awesome resume, and nice headshot does not create the person people want to be around and endorse; instead, it's all about attitude and actions. By embracing this reality, remaining true to ourselves, and selflessly serving others along the way, we'll forever be able to count on those we've met on our journey to stand with us in a crisis. *What are you doing to be the kind of leader and friend people fall in love with?*

## reflections and intentions

my thoughts and feelings on today's FLASHPOINTS include:

my intentions and action items today include:

today I am grateful for:

# Clear Desk = Clear Mind

When we're under pressure—when life and business seems to be swirling around us and everything seems to be happening at once—chances are, our desk or work area is looking disheveled, too. Working in a disorganized space can affect our ability to concentrate and reduce productivity. Let's try this: before we head home each day, we clear and organize our workspaces. We create a neat pile of any paperwork needed in the morning, file away anything possible, and get rid of any rubbish. When we arrive in the morning, even though we know we've got a lot to get through, it will be that much easier to start fresh, and we'll physically be able to focus on one task at a time. *Look around you now, what's your workspace look like?*

## reflections and intentions

my thoughts and feelings on today's FLASHPOINTS include:

my intentions and action items today include:

today I am grateful for:

# Forward this on to 10 people ... and something great will happen to you tomorrow.

I don't believe those emails we often receive, telling us that we need to forward the message to at least 10 people or something grave will happen in the next 24 hours. It's simply not logical ... and really, I'm a bit of a risk taker, anyway, so bring it on! The message may be nutty, but maybe there's some merit to the method. When was the last time we told our associates, clients and team that we appreciate them and the role they play in our lives? What if we sent a cheery "how are you?" email, without the chainmail sub-text, and we actually received that "something great" that's meant to be happening to us tomorrow, after all? *Do you dare to send out 10 thank you messages today?*

## reflections and intentions

my thoughts and feelings on today's FLASHPOINTS include:

my intentions and action items today include:

today I am grateful for:

> ## *Sometimes we stare so long at a door that is closing that we see too late the one that is open.*
>
> ### ~ Alexander Graham Bell

After five days of prompting and prodding new ideas and thoughts to come to mind, today we review what we've discovered. It's time to take a peek back at our journaling, to review our thoughts, feelings, and action items; and see how well we did. After all, self-awareness is the key to initiate growth and realize lasting change.

## weekly reflection

reflecting on my thoughts, feelings and experiences from this past week, the top three that impacted me the most include:

my top "ta-da's" (successes) from this past week include:

my top "oh-no's" (disappointments) from this past week include:

my top "ah-ha's" (discoveries) from this past week include:

> ## I don't believe in a fate that will fall on us no matter what we do. I do believe in a fate that will fall on us if we do nothing.
>
> ### ~ Ronald Reagan

The end of the week is the best time to plan for the coming week. And at this point, you've reviewed the previous week and can be prepared to make changes and take actions based on thought, not re-action. You want to keep your goals in mind always. So today is your opportunity to look at yesterday's Weekly Reflection and decide what you're going to do and when. It is most often small tweaks that will lead to great success, fueled by a positive and grateful attitude.

## weekly intentions

my top "go get-'em's" (fixes) to implement this coming week include:

incomplete action items, that support my goals, to carry over into this coming week include: (schedule them now and be specific.)

new action items, that support my goals, for this coming week include: (schedule them now and be specific.)

something new I'm grateful for this week, and with whom I will share it:

# RISK:
## if you win, you'll be happy;
## if you lose, you'll be wise.

Let's push the envelope a bit, and live a little! Happy or wise—either way, we're improving. I'm not talking about uncalculated risks that endanger our health or well-being. I'm more interested in risks associated with designing our ideal life, loving more deeply, or leading our dream business ... those key areas that impact our legacy and sphere of influence. Sure, it takes guts to forge past the doubts of others—I've been there. Sadly, though, great ideas are often lost to laughter and ridicule. Taking risks and failing is like losing our footing; but never taking risks is like losing ourselves. Having a *massive vision* for life, love and business, while risky, can soothe the barbs of ridicule and failure. *How big is your dream? Is it worth the risks?*

## reflections and intentions

my thoughts and feelings on today's FLASHPOINTS include:

my intentions and action items today include:

today I am grateful for:

## Knock, knock. Who's there?
## One new introduction could be all it takes.

Today's challenge: We must take time to introduce ourselves to people we'd normally walk right past. We might be genuinely surprised by who they are. That's right, we need to take risks and introduce ourselves to those we sit next to, the barista, or that neighbor we always see but don't know. What are their stories? How might we serve? What might we learn from them? These people are in our lives, yet we've probably never had a lengthy conversation with them, because we couldn't see their value to us. What if there was significant value there, but we just didn't know it yet? Would that change our desire to interact with them? *How many new friends can you make today, and what stories can you discover?*

### reflections and intentions

my thoughts and feelings on today's FLASHPOINTS include:

my intentions and action items today include:

today I am grateful for:

# I am the customer!

You're not just an entrepreneur, leader or executive—you're a consumer. With that in mind, how often do you use your own insights to fuel improvements in your business? It helps to imagine what you, as a consumer, would expect from your own business—from excellent customer service right through to the look and feel of your brand and marketing initiatives. How often do you challenge your team (and yourself, for that matter) to think from your customer's point of view? It's in the small, daily actions and interactions that your organization builds its profile and reputation in the community. *What organizational challenge can you identify, and how can you rejuvenate the mood of your team by thinking like your customer?*

## reflections and intentions

my thoughts and feelings on today's FLASHPOINTS include:

my intentions and action items today include:

today I am grateful for:

# When we're not measuring our economy in dollars, kindness is the real currency of titans.

The kindness of one to another goes much deeper than a brief personal exchange. Through an act of kindness, we attract further kindness to ourselves—it's one of those unexplainables that just *is*. Although completely controllable, we don't often consider If we want to be kind or not; it either happens or it doesn't. It seems so basic to consider kindness as a trait every entrepreneur and leader should possess—but perhaps it's in considering it that we remind ourselves of its value. If we're jerks to those around us, it won't matter how great our product or service is; loyalty, success and significance will elude us. Kindness creates kindness in others. *How can you work to show an increased level of kindness to just one person today?*

## reflections and intentions

my thoughts and feelings on today's FLASHPOINTS include:

my intentions and action items today include:

today I am grateful for:

## Sometimes our good ideas really ARE harebrained!

Could our latest business idea, its launch or operation be stuck in a rut? It's easy to get so excited about an idea that we dive headlong into it as a business before we've conducted due diligence on its viability or sustainability. What may be a deep personal interest or skill for us may not translate into a viable business. Consider this: not every good idea is meant to be a business opportunity to be launched and operated by ourselves. Run that idea or business model by several experienced, respected and emotionally detached entrepreneurs and business gurus for a reality check. Discretion is often the better part of valor. *Is your latest business idea better suited as a hobby? Either way, how do you know?*

### reflections and intentions

my thoughts and feelings on today's FLASHPOINTS include:

my intentions and action items today include:

today I am grateful for:

> ## Yes and No are very short words to say, but we should think for some length of time before saying them.
>
> ~ Anonymous

After five days of prompting and prodding new ideas and thoughts to come to mind, today we review what we've discovered. It's time to take a peek back at our journaling, to review our thoughts, feelings, and action items; and see how well we did. After all, self-awareness is the key to initiate growth and realize lasting change.

## weekly reflection

reflecting on my thoughts, feelings and experiences from this past week, the top three that impacted me the most include:

my top "ta-da's" (successes) from this past week include:

my top "oh-no's" (disappointments) from this past week include:

my top "ah-ha's" (discoveries) from this past week include:

> # In a networked world, trust is the most important currency.
> ~ Eric Schmidt

The end of the week is the best time to plan for the coming week. And at this point, you've reviewed the previous week and can be prepared to make changes and take actions based on thought, not re-action. You want to keep your goals in mind always. So today is your opportunity to look at yesterday's Weekly Reflection and decide what you're going to do and when. It is most often small tweaks that will lead to great success, fueled by a positive and grateful attitude.

## weekly intentions

my top "go get-'em's" (fixes) to implement this coming week include:

incomplete action items, that support my goals, to carry over into this coming week include: (schedule them now and be specific.)

new action items, that support my goals, for this coming week include: (schedule them now and be specific.)

something new I'm grateful for this week, and with whom I will share it:

## Attitude is everything!

Well, it may not be absolutely everything, but our attitude certainly affects our outcomes—our communications, actions, reputation and, most importantly, our opportunities. We often hear the saying "It's not what you know, but who you know." Imagine if someone we knew had a negative attitude about their business or some aspect of it. It's not likely you'd refer them to others. A genuinely positive attitude can boost your reputation among community leaders and stakeholders, attract and retain high achievers to your team, and create open and honest lines of communication. We're the chief role model of our organization, and we influence the attitude or our team. A good attitude won't guarantee victory, but a bad one will guarantee defeat. *What's your attitude saying about you?*

## reflections and intentions

my thoughts and feelings on today's FLASHPOINTS include:

my intentions and action items today include:

today I am grateful for:

# What you don't see with your eyes, don't witness with your mouth.

It's likely we've all worked in environments where behind-the-back gossip is rife and sometimes raw. Just because it's prevalent doesn't make it right ... or any easier to deal with. Here's how simple office communication should be: we have a problem to discuss or a comment to make, we go straight to the person it involves and address the issue. Although not as salacious or intriguing, it's much easier to solve a problem when we go directly to the source ... plus it protects morale, saves time and energy, and avoids blowing things out of proportion. When you're on the receiving end of gossip, it shows true fortitude and leadership to challenge opinions and deal only with the facts. *How do you deal with gossip in your life?*

## reflections and intentions

my thoughts and feelings on today's FLASHPOINTS include:

my intentions and action items today include:

today I am grateful for:

> # *Failure is simply the opportunity to begin again, this time more intelligently.*
>
> ### ~ Henry Ford

I couldn't have said it better myself, but I'll elaborate: what Ford highlights here is that failure can be a brand new start and should not be considered an unsuccessful end. Every mistake, every swerve off the path, every action we wish could be undone—all are learning opportunities in business, leadership, and life. I like that there's no swagger in Ford's tone, just the simple message that with some reflection and course correction along the way, we become wiser following every failure. What comes next is building up the courage to take that next attempt beyond failure. Ponder this for a moment: if we're not failing, we're not moving fast enough, nor getting close enough to our fullest potential. *Do you have the guts to embrace failure?*

## reflections and intentions

my thoughts and feelings on today's FLASHPOINTS include:

my intentions and action items today include:

today I am grateful for:

> *It takes 20 years to build a reputation and 5 minutes to ruin it. If you think about that, you'll do things differently.*
>
> ~ Warren Buffett

Now, there's a reminder for providing ethical leadership and exceptional service if ever there was one! Really, take a moment to think about what Buffet is saying. It takes just one indiscretion, just one serious misstep, to truly blow it all. No, it's not impossible to repair a reputation ... but it ain't easy. Since the day we've opened our businesses and long before we've ever accepted our first leadership roles, we've worked on building a strong, positive reputation, right? That reputation has helped grow our sphere of influence and allowed us to achieve more. It's important to preserve this reputation—after all, it's what people will remember long after we're gone. *It's called legacy. How well are you considering your legacy in all the actions you take?*

## reflections and intentions

my thoughts and feelings on today's FLASHPOINTS include:

my intentions and action items today include:

today I am grateful for:

## Keep your friends close, and your enemies closer.

Does the same rule apply in business? You're darn tootin' … but not in the vindictive sense. Most of us find it easier to hate our enemies, a.k.a competitors, than to bless them. Truthfully, though, the hate (i.e., fear) we direct at our competition only destroys us. We can only improve things for ourselves by wishing the best for others. As a leader, isn't better to spend time making more contacts rather than worrying about the competition? Of course! Being the bigger person and venturing over to meet a competitor could help gain an ally in the industry. It could also help bring future referrals, not to mention the possible realization that they're pretty great! *Are you a good sport in all areas of life? How so?*

## reflections and intentions

my thoughts and feelings on today's FLASHPOINTS include:

my intentions and action items today include:

today I am grateful for:

> # In the confrontation between the stream and the rock, the stream always wins, not through strength but by perseverance.
> ~ H. Jackson Brown

After five days of prompting and prodding new ideas and thoughts to come to mind, today we review what we've discovered. It's time to take a peek back at our journaling, to review our thoughts, feelings, and action items; and see how well we did. After all, self-awareness is the key to initiate growth and realize lasting change.

## weekly reflection

reflecting on my thoughts, feelings and experiences from this past week, the top three that impacted me the most include:

my top "ta-da's" (successes) from this past week include:

my top "oh-no's" (disappointments) from this past week include:

my top "ah-ha's" (discoveries) from this past week include:

> # *People do not decide to become extraordinary.*
> # *They decide to accomplish extraordinary things.*
> ## *~ Sir Edmund Hilary*

The end of the week is the best time to plan for the coming week. And at this point, you've reviewed the previous week and can be prepared to make changes and take actions based on thought, not re-action. You want to keep your goals in mind always. So today is your opportunity to look at yesterday's Weekly Reflection and decide what you're going to do and when. It is most often small tweaks that will lead to great success, fueled by a positive and grateful attitude.

## weekly intentions

my top "go get-'em's" (fixes) to implement this coming week include:

incomplete action items, that support my goals, to carry over into this coming week include: (schedule them now and be specific.)

new action items, that support my goals, for this coming week include: (schedule them now and be specific.)

something new I'm grateful for this week, and with whom I will share it:

# Work.
# Life.
# Balance?

Society has this idea that there's a magic formula for how much we should "work" and how much we should "play." Most high achievers merge the two—they accept the hard work and understand that changing the status quo often requires long hours. For some, the grueling quest is a rewarding experience that defines them. For others, after some time, the quest stops working and becomes a drain. The answer is not in searching for some magic formula but following instincts, being happy and doing what works for us *and* our family. If being a full-time entrepreneur works, great! Who is society to judge us? If it stops working, we need to change our habits and spend time doing other things that are enjoyable. *What rules are you setting about achievement?*

## reflections and intentions

my thoughts and feelings on today's FLASHPOINTS include:

my intentions and action items today include:

today I am grateful for:

# If you're looking for a new outlook or outcome in life, try this on for size: Serve others.

Let's start with this: there's no higher calling than serving others. Period. If you're looking to "up-level" your life or business, forget about "the secret" and "systems" the shysters are peddling. Whether you believe in religion, karma, self-development, or something entirely different, being of service to others is the only way to experience a life of significance *and* success. Service is not about forgetting our own goals in place of others' ... it's not even about charity. It's about the realization that the world is not all about us ... it's about the other people out there, and the contributions we can make in serving them. Grasping this simple truth will put your entire life into perspective. *When was the last time you served others with zero expectations of remuneration?*

## reflections and intentions

my thoughts and feelings on today's FLASHPOINTS include:

my intentions and action items today include:

today I am grateful for:

# Vision is the promise of what you shall one day become ...

Our personal and professional vision statement should excite and prove to be a resource to refuel, recharge and re-energize our efforts. Properly defined and crafted, a vision will assist in communicating our dreams and aspiration for our own future and that of our sphere of influence. A vision that inspires greatness is both positive and inspirational... defining what life could be. An awesome vision statement will inspire us every time we read it, attract superstars to join us on our quest and serve as a guide to shape future decisions to grow our life and business. *Does your vision for your future and the future of your team excite and inspire you to take action?*

## reflections and intentions

my thoughts and feelings on today's FLASHPOINTS include:

my intentions and action items today include:

today I am grateful for:

# The business of business is people ... without them, we're nothing.

If people really are our biggest asset, shouldn't we respect them? Associates, partners and advisors may have joined us because of our inspirational vision, but it's time to turn them into a highly functioning team to help launch or expand our project. Start by treating them the way we want our customers and clients to be treated. It's baffling to see managers and business owners treat their team like garbage, then expect them to turn around and serve their clients with a smile. We must create opportunities for our team to bond and develop a common purpose, allowing them to attend educational and personal development programs, treating them to lunches occasionally, and allowing them to participate in community projects. Growth WILL result! *How are you investing in your biggest asset?*

## reflections and intentions

my thoughts and feelings on today's FLASHPOINTS include:

my intentions and action items today include:

today I am grateful for:

> ## It's either risk everything and do something,
> ## or risk everything and do nothing.
>
> ~ Darrell Fusaro

Inaction is a common reaction to not knowing what step to take next. It's far easier and less risky to procrastinate and do nothing than to take the "wrong" step. Right? Wrong! Doing nothing or carrying on without taking risks or making changes will stunt our personal and professional growth. If we take that first tiny step, then take another, soon it gets easier to take chances and make changes, because we have momentum. So is doing nothing really easier or less risky than taking action? It might be easier in terms of decision-making, but it won't help us reach our goals any faster—in fact, quite the opposite. *Be truly honest: Is taking action and calculated risk an essential part of your daily diet?*

## reflections and intentions

my thoughts and feelings on today's FLASHPOINTS include:

my intentions and action items today include:

today I am grateful for:

> ## Man cannot discover new oceans unless he has the courage to lose sight of the shore.
>
> ### ~ Andre Gide

After five days of prompting and prodding new ideas and thoughts to come to mind, today we review what we've discovered. It's time to take a peek back at our journaling, to review our thoughts, feelings, and action items; and see how well we did. After all, self-awareness is the key to initiate growth and realize lasting change.

## weekly reflection

reflecting on my thoughts, feelings and experiences from this past week, the top three that impacted me the most include:

my top "ta-da's" (successes) from this past week include:

my top "oh-no's" (disappointments) from this past week include:

my top "ah-ha's" (discoveries) from this past week include:

> # How can there be so much difference between a day off and an off day?
>
> ~ Anonymous

The end of the week is the best time to plan for the coming week. And at this point, you've reviewed the previous week and can be prepared to make changes and take actions based on thought, not re-action. You want to keep your goals in mind always. So today is your opportunity to look at yesterday's Weekly Reflection and decide what you're going to do and when. It is most often small tweaks that will lead to great success, fueled by a positive and grateful attitude.

## weekly intentions

my top "go get-'em's" (fixes) to implement this coming week include:

incomplete action items, that support my goals, to carry over into this coming week include: (schedule them now and be specific.)

new action items, that support my goals, for this coming week include: (schedule them now and be specific.)

something new I'm grateful for this week, and with whom I will share it:

# Failure is so important to success, that it should have its own check-box on our to-do list.

It's through failure that we grow, learn and create. Failure itself is not noteworthy, but what we learn from the journey is. Let's say we host a gala fundraiser, and only 10 people show up (ouch!)—the achievement is in discovering how to increase attendance the next time. Perhaps we launch a new product, and sales are on the skids (d'oh!)—achievement is in identifying what can be improved, and then taking action: changes to the product or the way it's marketed, packaged or delivered. When failure is just another item on the to-do list, rather than cause for self-flagellation, our minds become open to endless possibilities and bold steps toward recovery and learning. *What projects will hit the "fail at something" category on your to-do list this week?*

## reflections and intentions

my thoughts and feelings on today's FLASHPOINTS include:

my intentions and action items today include:

today I am grateful for:

# You don't know what you don't know until you know you didn't know it ... you know?

Even after we've achieved much success in our career, business, and our relationships, there's still so much more to learn and achieve in life. Lifelong learning is the ticket to an open mind, infinite ideas and unimaginable opportunities. Every new lesson learned can help us see the world in a new light—and it's awesome! If we're feeling stumped for creativity or finding it difficult to focus on our ideas, maybe it's time to get out of our stale routines and take up a new learning opportunity. Perhaps it's time to infuse a new perspective by adding someone new to our team or personal in-crowd. *What opportunity to learn will you embark on next?*

## reflections and intentions

my thoughts and feelings on today's FLASHPOINTS include:

my intentions and action items today include:

today I am grateful for:

## Sharing is Caring.

Building more meaningful relationships with clients and customers means identifying our core values and genuinely communicating them. As consumers become more savvy, they expect their values to align with the businesses they deal with. Do you participate in your local community or serve the less fortunate? Do you give your staff time off to volunteer and access to education? No matter our view on corporate philanthropy, it's proven that support and active participation in causes that are of interest to our team improves productivity, morale, and loyalty. Let's not be shy about sharing our actions with clients and the public—customers who don't share our values may be turned off, but we'll build deeper, more meaningful relationships with those who do. *How do you share what's important to you?*

## reflections and intentions

my thoughts and feelings on today's FLASHPOINTS include:

my intentions and action items today include:

today I am grateful for:

## Analysis paralysis sucks.
## Action is power.

Among the many responsibilities of leaders and achievers is the ability to make sound decisions that are in the best interests of those in our charge (including ourselves). This involves a clear-headed thought process: a pros and cons list, collecting and deciphering information, asking profound questions, gut checks and, from time to time, trial and error. The specifics of the decision often don't matter (as there may be no clear right or wrong)—we just need to make a bold choice. What's most important, after a survey of the landscape, is to stop over-analyzing, push through the fear, and take decisive action. When we miss the mark or intended target, we must simply make course corrections along the way. *How can taking action change the trajectory of your success plan?*

## reflections and intentions

my thoughts and feelings on today's FLASHPOINTS include:

my intentions and action items today include:

today I am grateful for:

## Dude, don't be a buzz-kill!

Have you ever left an event positively buzzing after you met someone amazing? Yeah, me too. Surrounding ourselves with positive, encouraging people is key in keeping our own spirits up once the honeymoon of a new endeavor is over. Maybe it's because these people are reminders of better times, or they have inspiring, courageous stories to share, or they're simply a distraction from our own problems. Or maybe, just maybe, they're our cosmic reminder to pay it forward, to get out there and be the one who uplifts others. Take this challenge: stop pushing and shoving toward personal goals; rather, serve and uplift others in small and simple ways. We'll feel great, and they'll be inspired. *What are you so passionate about that the thought of it gets you buzzing?*

## reflections and intentions

my thoughts and feelings on today's FLASHPOINTS include:

my intentions and action items today include:

today I am grateful for:

> ## *Courage is not the absence of fear, but rather the judgment that something else is more important than fear.*
>
> ### ~ Ambrose Redmoon

After five days of prompting and prodding new ideas and thoughts to come to mind, today we review what we've discovered. It's time to take a peek back at our journaling, to review our thoughts, feelings, and action items; and see how well we did. After all, self-awareness is the key to initiate growth and realize lasting change.

## weekly reflection

reflecting on my thoughts, feelings and experiences from this past week, the top three that impacted me the most include:

my top "ta-da's" (successes) from this past week include:

my top "oh-no's" (disappointments) from this past week include:

my top "ah-ha's" (discoveries) from this past week include:

> ## It's not so much how busy you are, but why you are busy. The bee is praised. The mosquito is swatted.
>
> ### ~ Mary O'Connor

The end of the week is the best time to plan for the coming week. And at this point, you've reviewed the previous week and can be prepared to make changes and take actions based on thought, not re-action. You want to keep your goals in mind always. So today is your opportunity to look at yesterday's Weekly Reflection and decide what you're going to do and when. It is most often small tweaks that will lead to great success, fueled by a positive and grateful attitude.

## weekly intentions

my top "go get-'em's" (fixes) to implement this coming week include:

incomplete action items, that support my goals, to carry over into this coming week include: (schedule them now and be specific.)

new action items, that support my goals, for this coming week include: (schedule them now and be specific.)

something new I'm grateful for this week, and with whom I will share it:

## Customer satisfaction is pointless, but client loyalty is priceless!

Mere satisfaction is the slow death of every relationship. Online review forums buzz with negative banter of mediocre service standards that, left unchecked, will kill any organization. From the very moment of initial contact with a potential customer to long after they've experienced a service or product, exceeding expectations is the only way we'll build long-term loyal clients. World-class organizations design legendary service systems that focus on building fiercely loyal clients, enticing them to expand their relationship by seeking feedback, enhancing products and services based on what they've learned and keeping in touch long after the transaction ... all the while, offering assurance they've made the right decision in doing business with them. *What does your customer service process look like?*

## reflections and intentions

my thoughts and feelings on today's FLASHPOINTS include:

my intentions and action items today include:

today I am grateful for:

> # Only those who can see the invisible can do the impossible.

It's critical to have a clearly articulated, aspirational and inspiring vision for business and life. Equally important to the written mantra is playing the mental movie, by visualizing the journey and the attainment of our goals. If we don't believe it's possible and can't visualize it, how will we inspire and enlist others to join our cause? Olympians, warriors, peacemakers and empire builders have all used the power of visualization to achieve their goals. Here's how. Step 1: Create an inspiring vision. Step 2: Believe it! Step 3: Visualize every detail of what success looks, sounds and smells like. Step 4: Play the mental movie over and over, several times every day. Step 5: Take action to make it so. *In what ways are you prepared to do the impossible?*

## reflections and intentions

my thoughts and feelings on today's FLASHPOINTS include:

my intentions and action items today include:

today I am grateful for:

# Finish this sentence:
# I love working with clients who...

One of the most interesting things about business and leadership is the array of characters and clients we work with each day. Think of an ideal client—what makes them a favorite? Are they easy to work with? Are they respectful communicators who express their appreciation? Perhaps it's their big budget—that's always nice! Whatever it is, how can we morph the most challenging clients into our favorites? Start by asking specific questions to get to each other's hot button issues (like inquiring about budget constraints) and define communication styles that are acceptable so that expectations are met. After all, if people don't know our expectations, they'll never meet them. When we take responsibility, we make every experience more positive. *How will you approach working with your next client?*

## reflections and intentions

my thoughts and feelings on today's FLASHPOINTS include:

my intentions and action items today include:

today I am grateful for:

# Fear.
# The real four letter word.

We're all walking around with the same fears inside us—it's just that some choose to face them head on. Imagine that tense situation you hate to be put in—introducing yourself to a roomful of people you don't know, heading a meeting with a potential new investor, making a big financial decision where you can't foresee the results...the list goes on. The difference between a high achiever and an average Joe is that the achiever finds the courage to face fears and challenge them, time after time. Fear lives in us all, and how we deal with it is what makes or breaks our success. Remember this: in life, there is no use for inaction or cowardice. What's your relationship to fear?

## reflections and intentions

my thoughts and feelings on today's FLASHPOINTS include:

my intentions and action items today include:

today I am grateful for:

> # With health comes hope, with hope comes optimism, with optimism comes opportunity.

High achievement is demanding on the mind *and* body, so it helps to make physical *and* mental health a priority among all our other to-dos. We've heard it before: sleep deprivation reduces alertness, busyness leads to errors and lack of emotional freedom reduces creativity. Yet, too many of us wear "overwhelmed" as a badge of honor. To improve hope and health, breathe, take short breaks often and find joy throughout the day. To reduce stress, try this: establish "do not disturb" time during the day for 30 minutes of focus/quiet time and commit to some form of physical activity you enjoy a few times each week ... endorphins released during physical exercise lead to a more optimistic and upbeat mood. *How will you exercise your mind and body today?*

## reflections and intentions

my thoughts and feelings on today's FLASHPOINTS include:

my intentions and action items today include:

today I am grateful for:

> # *A man is only as big as what he lets distract him.*
>
> ## ~ John D. Smetzer III

After five days of prompting and prodding new ideas and thoughts to come to mind, today we review what we've discovered. It's time to take a peek back at our journaling, to review our thoughts, feelings, and action items; and see how well we did. After all, self-awareness is the key to initiate growth and realize lasting change.

## weekly reflection

reflecting on my thoughts, feelings and experiences from this past week, the top three that impacted me the most include:

my top "ta-da's" (successes) from this past week include:

my top "oh-no's" (disappointments) from this past week include:

my top "ah-ha's" (discoveries) from this past week include:

> ## *If you put off everything till you're sure of it, you'll never get anything done.*
> ~ Norman Vincent Peale

The end of the week is the best time to plan for the coming week. And at this point, you've reviewed the previous week and can be prepared to make changes and take actions based on thought, not re-action. You want to keep your goals in mind always. So today is your opportunity to look at yesterday's Weekly Reflection and decide what you're going to do and when. It is most often small tweaks that will lead to great success, fueled by a positive and grateful attitude.

## weekly intentions

my top "go get-'em's" (fixes) to implement this coming week include:

incomplete action items, that support my goals, to carry over into this coming week include: (schedule them now and be specific.)

new action items, that support my goals, for this coming week include: (schedule them now and be specific.)

something new I'm grateful for this week, and with whom I will share it:

# When you're too busy to help those around you succeed, you're too busy.

"I'm just so busy!" is a common complaint and constant struggle for many of us—after all, they don't call it "busi-ness" for nothing! Okay, so we've heard it all before—being a leader of any organization is no 9-to-5 gig. The responsibilities and never-ending lists of to-dos can drain our lifeblood. But now is not the time to isolate and neglect our team. It is, after all, our team that pushes through all the roadblocks and obstacles to support us. So keep some energy in reserve to spur them on toward greatness, too. *Is busy-ness a reality of your business, or is it just a state of mind that could do with some re-programming? What's your relationship to being busy?*

## reflections and intentions

my thoughts and feelings on today's FLASHPOINTS include:

my intentions and action items today include:

today I am grateful for:

# When the fog of chaos clears, the clarity of a more promising path comes into view.

Conventional wisdom says we become more settled with age, and our career paths just seem to organically sort themselves out. Yet it's estimated that a person will hold any given job for just over four years. Considering the number of years in the workforce, that's a lot of migration! While the number of career changes may be fewer for entrepreneurs and business owners, it's still common to move from one venture to another. The reality is, change is constant and no one has it all figured out ... nor do they need to. Those who have found emotional nirvana expect, embrace and learn from change. When we stop enjoying what we do, it's time to move on! *In what areas of life do you feel the winds of change blowing?*

## reflections and intentions

my thoughts and feelings on today's FLASHPOINTS include:

my intentions and action items today include:

today I am grateful for:

## Trust is like an eraser.
## Without integrity, it gets smaller and
## smaller with each misstep.

Personal trust and integrity are important across all areas of our lives: relationally, spiritually, emotionally, and professionally. We either live by these traits and tenants, or not—if we're honest with ourselves, there's no in between that makes any real sense. Wikipedia tells us, "Integrity is a concept of consistency of actions, values, methods, measures, principles, expectations and outcomes." Integrity is the quality of having an intuitive sense of honesty and truthfulness about our motivations and actions that creates enduring success and lasting significance. We find it much easier to trust those folks who actually live with integrity than those who simply pay lip service. *How are you faring on the quest for integrity, honesty and consistency?*

## reflections and intentions

my thoughts and feelings on today's FLASHPOINTS include:

my intentions and action items today include:

today I am grateful for:

# Do as I say, not as I do.

Sound familiar? Ever coached someone through a crisis, then realized you should take your own advice? That realization may prove to be a personal moment of Zen. As leaders and mentors, we can suddenly hear ourselves saying "just put one foot In front of the other and you'll get there," or "I know you're doing your best with the resources you have, so that's all I can expect of you." How often do we afford ourselves this forgiveness and understanding? Yes, we've all been crunched for time and driven for increased productivity with limited resources. So when we find ourselves in this position, it's best to start by taking our own advice. *In what area are you not practicing what you preach? Maybe the area in which you're most struggling?*

## reflections and intentions

my thoughts and feelings on today's FLASHPOINTS include:

my intentions and action items today include:

today I am grateful for:

## Get out of that sour mood.
## Your opportunities could change any second!

I received an unexpected call recently that completely changed the tone of my week. It reminded me that when we serve others without expectation of outcome or compensation, when we get out and mingle with people without fear of embarrassment, and when we dare to put our name forward for various opportunities and projects, our hard work and pursuit of excellence eventually pays off. Even if it's not how we expected it to ... which makes it doubly exciting! You may be having an awful day, week, month, season or year, but your opportunities could change at any moment. Don't allow a bad mood to repel your destiny. *So, will you dwell on the negatives, or will you brush them off and continue your journey toward a remarkable life?*

## reflections and intentions

my thoughts and feelings on today's FLASHPOINTS include:

my intentions and action items today include:

today I am grateful for:

> # When you go the extra mile you are seldom delayed by a traffic jam.
> ## ~ Zig Ziglar

After five days of prompting and prodding new ideas and thoughts to come to mind, today we review what we've discovered. It's time to take a peek back at our journaling, to review our thoughts, feelings, and action items; and see how well we did. After all, self-awareness is the key to initiate growth and realize lasting change.

## weekly reflection

reflecting on my thoughts, feelings and experiences from this past week, the top three that impacted me the most include:

my top "ta-da's" (successes) from this past week include:

my top "oh-no's" (disappointments) from this past week include:

my top "ah-ha's" (discoveries) from this past week include:

> # *Talk is cheap because supply exceeds demand.*
> ### ~ Anonymous

The end of the week is the best time to plan for the coming week. And at this point, you've reviewed the previous week and can be prepared to make changes and take actions based on thought, not re-action. You want to keep your goals in mind always. So today is your opportunity to look at yesterday's Weekly Reflection and decide what you're going to do and when. It is most often small tweaks that will lead to great success, fueled by a positive and grateful attitude.

## weekly intentions

my top "go get-'em's" (fixes) to implement this coming week include:

incomplete action items, that support my goals, to carry over into this coming week include: (schedule them now and be specific.)

new action items, that support my goals, for this coming week include: (schedule them now and be specific.)

something new I'm grateful for this week, and with whom I will share it:

# Leaders are not morally bound to infuse others with greatness. The greatness of leaders, however, taps the fountain of greatness found deep within us all.

At some point on our journey, we'll find ourselves questioning who we are and whether we've made the right choices. Sure, it helps at times to reflect and be critical, as this can sharpen our edge, create positive change and foster new opportunities. But, before getting too critical, remember there's honor in strong and selfless leadership. Be sure not to think too much about how things could've been if choices had been made differently. It's a destructive waste of time, and there's no going back to change what happened yesterday. Instead, look toward the future: we must take responsibility for the choices we will make and keep reminding ourselves of the privilege it is to be a leader. How peaceful are you with your leadership style?

## reflections and intentions

my thoughts and feelings on today's FLASHPOINTS include:

my intentions and action items today include:

today I am grateful for:

# Timing, tenacity and 10 years of trying will eventually make you an overnight success.

It's always interesting to read success stories of people and businesses that are painted to have become an "overnight success." In business, as in life, perseverance is key to making it really big. Few stars in business, sports, music or life can say they achieved success easily or overnight. For most of us, it takes years of hard work, bridge-building with the right people and developing an elite team to support our efforts and ideas. In short, success must be *earned*. While it's inspiring to hear these overnight success stories, there's no denying that they are the minority of cases. *How do you rate yourself on the stick-to-it-iveness-o-meter?*

## reflections and intentions

my thoughts and feelings on today's FLASHPOINTS include:

my intentions and action items today include:

today I am grateful for:

# Don't mistake others' limitations and failings for lack of standards. Communicate. Inspect. Expect.

As high achievers and leaders, we hold ourselves to a high standard. So why wouldn't we hold our teammates to that same standard? Our role as chief standard-bearer is vital to our venture's success, because our mission is to build the best product, service and team possible. But, slow down ... our expectations of high standards might prove detrimental to success if all we do is simply expect our teams to conform to high standards. Folks can't *meet* our expectations if they don't *know* our expectations. Progress starts with accessing the talent and resources of our team, effectively communicating our vision to inspire them, and encouraging them to bring their own ideas and flavors to the table. *How do you seek input for growth and excellence from your team?*

## reflections and intentions

my thoughts and feelings on today's FLASHPOINTS include:

my intentions and action items today include:

today I am grateful for:

> # When you really believe in your vision, you can't stop talking about it. So, if you've been quiet for a while, something's up.

Have you been so busy that it's keeping you quiet ... or is there some emotional, resource, or financial barrier in your way? I know, it's hard to be honest with ourselves when there's so much at stake. But, are you inspired by your life and goals? Yes? Then share your story! Not inspired? Not to worry. By cutting ourselves some slack, hitting our emotional reset buttons and redeploying our time, talent, and resources, we can get back on track. Now's the time to reflect and redefine our goals so that we're still invested in them. To face our fears about being the Chief Evangelist Officer (CEO) of our brands. To accept that we're only as great as the actions we take. *So, feel like talking now?*

## reflections and intentions

my thoughts and feelings on today's FLASHPOINTS include:

my intentions and action items today include:

today I am grateful for:

# iLISTEN.
# iLEARN.
# iLEAD.

Sure, we might be leaders, but we don't have all the answers all the time. Leadership involves listening, collaboration, partnerships and team building. Yes, we may very well be the go-to, answer person; but it's likely our teammates have the answers within themselves already. This is interesting for two reasons: Firstly, because, contrary to popular belief, leaders don't have all the answers, even though they attract all the questions (and problems)! Secondly, it should come as a big relief that, as a leader, all we actually need to do well is empower our teams to believe in themselves and their own judgment. It sure takes the pressure off having to be right all the time, doesn't it? *How do you bring out the best in those around you?*

## reflections and intentions

my thoughts and feelings on today's FLASHPOINTS include:

my intentions and action items today include:

today I am grateful for:

> # We do not stop playing because we grow old; we grow old because we stop playing.
> ~ Benjamin Franklin

After five days of prompting and prodding new ideas and thoughts to come to mind, today we review what we've discovered. It's time to take a peek back at our journaling, to review our thoughts, feelings, and action items; and see how well we did. After all, self-awareness is the key to initiate growth and realize lasting change.

## weekly reflection

reflecting on my thoughts, feelings and experiences from this past week, the top three that impacted me the most include:

my top "ta-da's" (successes) from this past week include:

my top "oh-no's" (disappointments) from this past week include:

my top "ah-ha's" (discoveries) from this past week include:

> ## *Courage is being scared to death, but saddling up anyway.*
> ### ~ John Wayne

The end of the week is the best time to plan for the coming week. And at this point, you've reviewed the previous week and can be prepared to make changes and take actions based on thought, not re-action. You want to keep your goals in mind always. So today is your opportunity to look at yesterday's Weekly Reflection and decide what you're going to do and when. It is most often small tweaks that will lead to great success, fueled by a positive and grateful attitude.

## weekly intentions

my top "go get-'em's" (fixes) to implement this coming week include:

incomplete action items, that support my goals, to carry over into this coming week include: (schedule them now and be specific.)

new action items, that support my goals, for this coming week include: (schedule them now and be specific.)

something new I'm grateful for this week, and with whom I will share it:

# Honestly,
# Honesty is vital to any endeavor.

It seems more than ever, consumers are looking for transparency from the organizations and brands they interact with. So, in response, organizations are being more open about their financial condition and corporate culture—at least for those who pride themselves in providing an honest, morally sound, and socially good service or product. Answer this: *How much focus and energy is placed on honesty in your organization? Are you willing to open your books, systems, and even workplace environment and invite the public right in?* If not, the very things we try to hide are probably the things that are holding us back, without us even realizing it. The challenge remains: spend energy on the things that matter, rather than trying to hide. *Where can you incorporate more transparency?*

## reflections and intentions

my thoughts and feelings on today's FLASHPOINTS include:

my intentions and action items today include:

today I am grateful for:

# Improvement is elusive unless we set our eyes on a standard that's higher or better than our current state.

If put on the spot, we could all probably offer a short list of world-famous leadership, business and community role models without much difficulty. But many of us shy away from having such "world-class" mentors because they're simply not approachable or because we're searching for the perfect person (who doesn't exist). We find wise, inspirational figures closer to home, in the form of parents, siblings, colleagues, and even bosses. With "homegrown heroes" to look up to, having a mentor is always possible. And don't let geography or time zones prevent a mentor meeting—technology really can bend the space-time continuum. Let this serve as encouragement to raise the bar, and find a mentor this week. *Why admire role models from afar when your mentor may be in the next room?*

## reflections and intentions

my thoughts and feelings on today's FLASHPOINTS include:

my intentions and action items today include:

today I am grateful for:

> # *Where there is no vision the people will perish.*
>
> ## ~ Proverbs, 29:18

This is as true for organizations and companies as it is for communities and countries. As leaders and achievers, we must develop a crystal-clear vision of where we want to take our organization, while simultaneously inspiring action to make it a reality. Without action, our vision remains a dream. Having clarity around our vision and spreading that message far and wide will attract the right team members, clients, vendors and investors. When organizations veer off course, it's frequently because the leadership has muddied the vision or stopped effectively communicating the message to their sphere of influence. *How are you inspiring the power and energy to activate your vision?*

## reflections and intentions

my thoughts and feelings on today's FLASHPOINTS include:

my intentions and action items today include:

today I am grateful for:

## Once you find fun, fulfillment and joy in your "work," you'll add five days of living to every week.

No matter the nature of your calling or vocation, when it stops being fun, it suddenly becomes work. Let's face it, many of us spend more time at the office or on the road than we do in our homes. This leads me to believe that if we're investing so much time and energy into our professional pursuits, we should be reaping significant returns—in the form of fun! It's no secret that when people enjoy what they're doing, they're more fulfilled, dedicated and hardworking—and this is what leads to extraordinary team member engagement and, ultimately, stellar customer service. *How can you inject fun and fulfillment into the day for you and your team?*

## reflections and intentions

my thoughts and feelings on today's FLASHPOINTS include:

my intentions and action items today include:

today I am grateful for:

## The concept of teamwork is certainly not new. Maybe that's the lesson to be learned.

Teamwork is one of those brilliant methods that, if executed well, can turn our one-person dream into a sequence of actions hurtling quickly toward success. In fact, one of the fastest ways to gain momentum for turning that dream into reality is to enroll others in the vision, allow them to participate and excel, and then simply lead. These are the basics that effective leaders have used to build elite teams for thousands of years. There's a Special Operations maxim that says, "Individuals play the game, but teams beat the odds." *When was the last time you enlisted the help of others to accomplish your goals or took a personal interest in the development and solidarity of your team?*

## reflections and intentions

my thoughts and feelings on today's FLASHPOINTS include:

my intentions and action items today include:

today I am grateful for:

> ## *Let us endeavor so to live that when we come to die even the undertaker will be sorry.*
>
> ### ~ Mark Twain

After five days of prompting and prodding new ideas and thoughts to come to mind, today we review what we've discovered. It's time to take a peek back at our journaling, to review our thoughts, feelings, and action items; and see how well we did. After all, self-awareness is the key to initiate growth and realize lasting change.

## weekly reflection

reflecting on my thoughts, feelings and experiences from this past week, the top three that impacted me the most include:

my top "ta-da's" (successes) from this past week include:

my top "oh-no's" (disappointments) from this past week include:

my top "ah-ha's" (discoveries) from this past week include:

> ## *Live out of your imagination, not your history.*
> ### ~ Stephen Covey

The end of the week is the best time to plan for the coming week. And at this point, you've reviewed the previous week and can be prepared to make changes and take actions based on thought, not re-action. You want to keep your goals in mind always. So today is your opportunity to look at yesterday's Weekly Reflection and decide what you're going to do and when. It is most often small tweaks that will lead to great success, fueled by a positive and grateful attitude.

## weekly intentions

my top "go get-'em's" (fixes) to implement this coming week include:

incomplete action items, that support my goals, to carry over into this coming week include: (schedule them now and be specific.)

new action items, that support my goals, for this coming week include: (schedule them now and be specific.)

something new I'm grateful for this week, and with whom I will share it:

## The other to-do list: the "ta-da!" list.

Some of us make our to-do lists in the morning. Some list everything right before bed, then we wake up during the night and add more. There are entire seminars on how to formulate and use our to-do lists to be maximally productive. But sometimes our to-do lists are too long, too complicated, far too ambitious and downright overwhelming. And so items fall to the bottom of the pile and we simply "do the best we can." How about a different approach? Introducing the other to-do list: the "ta-da!" list. At the end of each day, after dinner but before bedtime, take a few moments to celebrate. You got things done today. Put them on the "ta-da!" list. *Give yourself credit, because you deserve it. What's your ta-da today?*

## reflections and intentions

my thoughts and feelings on today's FLASHPOINTS include:

my intentions and action items today include:

today I am grateful for:

# No one likes a salesperson, so stop selling!

Ok, that might be extreme, but there's an appropriate time and place to pitch your service or product; and networking events offer neither. Too often, we have an underlying agenda in which we're after something and usually want the people we meet to help us in some way. This might be fair, but going to a networking event and spending all our time trying to "sell" isn't useful and, frankly, is counterproductive. Don't do it! No one goes to networking events to buy, so don't sell. Instead, get to know people and serve those you meet. Serving is the best way to build relationships, and people buy from those with whom they have relationships. *Stop selling, and start serving. In what ways can you serve those you meet this week?*

## reflections and intentions

my thoughts and feelings on today's FLASHPOINTS include:

my intentions and action items today include:

today I am grateful for:

> *What makes a king out of a slave? Courage!*
> *What makes the flag on the mast to wave? Courage!*
> *What makes the elephant charge his tusk in the misty mist,*
> *or the dusky dusk?*
>
> ~ Cowardly Lion, Wizard of Oz

I was once accused of being naïve about making integrity, trust and compassion the core values of my business. I contend that courage provides the strength to be compassionate and the wisdom to be humble. Courage sustains us on our journey toward our dreams and visions. Courage allows us to care deeply and communicate effectively. It helps us drive on in the face of lingering doubt, push forward during bad economic conditions, and face our fears and dare to fail … failure is a key ingredient to success. At its root, integrity is based on courage. Without courage we're impotent and don't deserve the honor of being called "leader." *In what areas of your life should you be digging deep to summon more courage? "Courage. Ain't it the truth?"*

## reflections and intentions

my thoughts and feelings on today's FLASHPOINTS include:

my intentions and action items today include:

today I am grateful for:

# Bolder and brighter.

The ideas we exchange; the tidbits of wisdom we learn from family, friends and co-workers; the encouragement and growth we experience through interacting with others—all of these shape who we become in life. It's no surprise, then, that I'm a huge advocate of surrounding ourselves with positive and supportive people who become sounding boards for our ideas. People who teach, inspire and coach us out of our comfort zone and toward our fullest potential. Building this environment often means culling someone who's been "close" to us and replacing them with a community full of cheerleaders, mentors and sages who help keep our dream alive and well. *Of those you consider bolder and brighter than you, whom can you choose to surround yourself with?*

## reflections and intentions

my thoughts and feelings on today's FLASHPOINTS include:

my intentions and action items today include:

today I am grateful for:

## If you're not failing, you're not moving fast enough or coming close enough to your fullest potential.

Most of us won't realize our potential in life because we're paralyzed by fear. Fear can debilitate us if we let it … preventing us from dreaming big, placing limits on achievements by diminishing belief in ourselves and causing us to second-guess brilliant ideas because of possible embarrassment associated with failure. Reflect briefly on all the unmet potential resting in graveyards around the world. What if we dared to believe that *anything* is possible? What if the root of our focus and actions was the burning desire to reach our *fullest* potential? We'd be among the highest of high achievers who embrace and learn from failure, yet keep running toward our potential! Failure—expect it, embrace it and learn from it. *Where is fear keeping you from your fullest potential?*

## reflections and intentions

my thoughts and feelings on today's FLASHPOINTS include:

my intentions and action items today include:

today I am grateful for:

> ## *Try not to become a man of success but rather try to become a man of value.*
>
> ### ~ Albert Einstein

After five days of prompting and prodding new ideas and thoughts to come to mind, today we review what we've discovered. It's time to take a peek back at our journaling, to review our thoughts, feelings, and action items; and see how well we did. After all, self-awareness is the key to initiate growth and realize lasting change.

## weekly reflection

reflecting on my thoughts, feelings and experiences from this past week, the top three that impacted me the most include:

my top "ta-da's" (successes) from this past week include:

my top "oh-no's" (disappointments) from this past week include:

my top "ah-ha's" (discoveries) from this past week include:

> # *Too many people overvalue what they are not and undervalue what they are.*
> ## ~ Malcolm Forbes

The end of the week is the best time to plan for the coming week. And at this point, you've reviewed the previous week and can be prepared to make changes and take actions based on thought, not re-action. You want to keep your goals in mind always. So today is your opportunity to look at yesterday's Weekly Reflection and decide what you're going to do and when. It is most often small tweaks that will lead to great success, fueled by a positive and grateful attitude.

## weekly intentions

my top "go get-'em's" (fixes) to implement this coming week include:

incomplete action items, that support my goals, to carry over into this coming week include: (schedule them now and be specific.)

new action items, that support my goals, for this coming week include: (schedule them now and be specific.)

something new I'm grateful for this week, and with whom I will share it:

# Want victory in your business or leadership pursuits? First, create fiercely loyal fans.

At the core of every endeavor is the beneficiary: the recipient, the customer, or the team members in our charge. No matter who they are or their exact relationship with us, they're impacted by our decisions, efforts, values and value proposition. They become the beneficiaries of our problem solving skills, our vision, our savvy and our tenacity. We must recognize their worth because our level of success is directly proportional to the level of engagement and loyalty of these folks. Let's reflect on how we can more actively engage our fan base. It can be as simple as asking their opinion, offering a small "thank you discount," or publishing a newsletter with relevant and useful tips … the possibilities are endless! *How do you continue engaging your fan base?*

## reflections and intentions

my thoughts and feelings on today's FLASHPOINTS include:

my intentions and action items today include:

today I am grateful for:

## Commit entirely, live out your passions, and go full steam ahead!

I often write about conducting reconnaissance on our competitors in business—maybe that's because it's often our competition that drives us to do more and achieve more. In truth, if we want to be recognized as an industry leader, and if we want our business to succeed no matter what the competition is up to, we've got to go all in. Have I told you lately that super-achievement isn't easy? There are no ifs, buts, or maybes allowed. Full focus, passion, energy, and dedication are required. This doesn't mean we can't have other interests or areas of importance in life (to the contrary!), but when we have our business hat on, we must pull it down tight ... and put on a matching outfit. *Are you going full steam ahead?*

## reflections and intentions

my thoughts and feelings on today's FLASHPOINTS include:

my intentions and action items today include:

today I am grateful for:

# Saying "thank you" is more than good manners, it's good karma.

When was the last time you thanked a client for the opportunity to work with them? I'm not talking about saying "please" and "thank you" during over-the-counter transactions; that's merely being polite. I'm talking about expressing your gratitude for the opportunity to impact someone else's life, business and livelihood. If we truly appreciate those who make our cash registers ring, then we should speak up, because silent gratitude never serves anyone well. Too often we become so consumed with the transaction part of business, making the sale and meeting goals, that we forget to appreciate the opportunity to actually make a difference in someone's life. Isn't it amazing, and absolutely rewarding, to serve? *How do you show your gratitude and share that gratitude with your clients?*

## reflections and intentions

my thoughts and feelings on today's FLASHPOINTS include:

my intentions and action items today include:

today I am grateful for:

# From little things, big things grow.

When was the last time you reflected on the beginnings of your venture or most recent project? It seems that as we progress in business and life, we expect things to grow bigger and faster … which just might help us reach those goals we cherish much sooner. But, unfortunately, it's not the way most things pan out. We need to think back to our beginnings and realize how small and humble they were. Even if we are still in the early stages of our venture now, plenty of learning and achieving has occurred and there's much to be grateful for. So take a moment to stop, reflect and be grateful. *Where did you start? How have you grown? What have you learned through your successes … and failures?*

## reflections and intentions

my thoughts and feelings on today's FLASHPOINTS include:

my intentions and action items today include:

today I am grateful for:

## The biggest problem with email is the illusion that it's communication.

Emailing has certainly sped up decision making in the workplace, but is it really the most effective way to communicate with our team? I can think of hundreds of scenarios where emailing has made life easier for leaders and achievers—saving time and resources. There are, however, times when email causes more problems than it solves. For example, we can't easily communicate genuine excitement or passion with it. Emotions and feelings don't always translate accurately, and this can become a barrier for motivating and inspiring our team. That barely coherent email we sent our assistant late last night could have been communicated better in person, by phone, or video chat this morning, couldn't it? *Before you hit send, ask, "Is there a better way to communicate this more effectively?"*

### reflections and intentions

my thoughts and feelings on today's FLASHPOINTS include:

my intentions and action items today include:

today I am grateful for:

> ## The only limit to our realization of tomorrow will be our doubts of today.
> ### ~ Franklin Delano Roosevelt

After five days of prompting and prodding new ideas and thoughts to come to mind, today we review what we've discovered. It's time to take a peek back at our journaling, to review our thoughts, feelings, and action items; and see how well we did. After all, self-awareness is the key to initiate growth and realize lasting change.

## weekly reflection

reflecting on my thoughts, feelings and experiences from this past week, the top three that impacted me the most include:

my top "ta-da's" (successes) from this past week include:

my top "oh-no's" (disappointments) from this past week include:

my top "ah-ha's" (discoveries) from this past week include:

> ## Strength does not come from physical capacity. It comes from an indomitable will.
> ### ~ Mohandas Gandhi

The end of the week is the best time to plan for the coming week. And at this point, you've reviewed the previous week and can be prepared to make changes and take actions based on thought, not re-action. You want to keep your goals in mind always. So today is your opportunity to look at yesterday's Weekly Reflection and decide what you're going to do and when. It is most often small tweaks that will lead to great success, fueled by a positive and grateful attitude.

## weekly intentions

my top "go get-'em's" (fixes) to implement this coming week include:

incomplete action items, that support my goals, to carry over into this coming week include: (schedule them now and be specific.)

new action items, that support my goals, for this coming week include: (schedule them now and be specific.)

something new I'm grateful for this week, and with whom I will share it:

## The key to surrounding yourself with positive, loyal and honest people is to be one of those people.

In love and nature, we tend to believe that opposites attract. When it comes to core values and goal setting, however, like attracts like—it's one of the principles by which many of us choose to live. If we want to be surrounded by people who are in big business, we must have that goal for ourselves and our business. So think BIG! To be surrounded by people who are socially responsible in business, we must look at our OWN business and see what changes must be made to be more socially responsible. And likewise, to attract friends and teammates who are loyal and honest, we must display these traits first. *What, and whom, are you attracting through your character traits?*

## reflections and intentions

my thoughts and feelings on today's FLASHPOINTS include:

my intentions and action items today include:

today I am grateful for:

> # Poor communication damages relationships and limits growth. Effective communication is the language of leadership.

When it comes to communication, simplicity works best. To effectively improve loyalty, relationships and growth through communication, we must leave our industry jargon and hyperbole at the door. When we over-communicate while introducing ourselves or when describing our products and services, people get confused. Remember this: confused minds don't buy. So, keep it simple. To simplify how you describe the benefits of your service or product, present them as if you're communicating with a child. Kids have an amazing ability to be genuinely straightforward and simplistic, don't they? We could all learn a little from them. Stick to using language most people can understand—that way, our message can reach our audience in a way they can actually relate to. *How simply can you describe your products and services?*

## reflections and intentions

my thoughts and feelings on today's FLASHPOINTS include:

my intentions and action items today include:

today I am grateful for:

# Passion ignites the fire in our bellies and drives us to dream of expanded horizons beyond our fears and failures.

Everyone on our team has a particular role and each has their own personal passion. It's these passions and interests that we must identify to create a team that is totally on fire! What is it that attracted our team members to their particular roles? Is it direct customer interaction? Writing? Finding creative solutions? Ask them! When our roles evolve in business, sometimes the very thing that excited us to begin with is no longer a focus. As a leader, it's our task to ensure each member of our team is successful—one of the best ways to do this is to create an environment where they are in love with their roles and working in their strengths and passion. *What are your team members passionate about?*

## reflections and intentions

my thoughts and feelings on today's FLASHPOINTS include:

my intentions and action items today include:

today I am grateful for:

## Innovation flourishes when grand ideation meets bold action.

Ingenious ideas are often born from challenges we'd like to overcome or opportunities we'd like to seize. If ideation and innovation aren't really our thing, we need to enlist blue-sky thinkers to brainstorm about our desired outcome. Good ideas often come from bad ones or from ideas that were good once upon a time but are no longer viable. Generating grand ideas and fostering an environment of innovation begins with a positive, can-do attitude ... we need to check reality at the door and have fun. Start small, if necessary, but shake things up and try a new approach whenever possible. Here's an idea: let's try taking a different route to work tomorrow and see what we'll learn. *What old idea, turned new, could breathe new life into your life?*

## reflections and intentions

my thoughts and feelings on today's FLASHPOINTS include:

my intentions and action items today include:

today I am grateful for:

## Did curiosity really kill the cat?

I overheard a news story discussing the need for adults to nurture the curiosity of infants to stimulate the baby's emotional growth and development. It made me ask, "Does this curiosity ever ease as we age?" While our curiosities change with age and experience, it seems that human nature drives us to continually ask questions, seek answers, and to be on a constant quest to experience new things. Why not nurture this curiosity in every area of life, including our place of work? I encourage you to encourage your team to take on skill enriching extracurricular activities outside the workplace! I'll bet you'll find increased professional engagement and innovation, deeper personal satisfaction and happier team members. *How can you inspire greater curiosity among your team?*

## reflections and intentions

my thoughts and feelings on today's FLASHPOINTS include:

my intentions and action items today include:

today I am grateful for:

> *Replace the word 'problem' with the word 'opportunity' in all your thoughts.*
>
> ~ Matthew Keith Groves

After five days of prompting and prodding new ideas and thoughts to come to mind, today we review what we've discovered. It's time to take a peek back at our journaling, to review our thoughts, feelings, and action items; and see how well we did. After all, self-awareness is the key to initiate growth and realize lasting change.

## weekly reflection

reflecting on my thoughts, feelings and experiences from this past week, the top three that impacted me the most include:

my top "ta-da's" (successes) from this past week include:

my top "oh-no's" (disappointments) from this past week include:

my top "ah-ha's" (discoveries) from this past week include:

*Common sense is genius
dressed up in work clothes.*
~ Ralph Waldo Emerson

The end of the week is the best time to plan for the coming week. And at this point, you've reviewed the previous week and can be prepared to make changes and take actions based on thought, not re-action. You want to keep your goals in mind always. So today is your opportunity to look at yesterday's Weekly Reflection and decide what you're going to do and when. It is most often small tweaks that will lead to great success, fueled by a positive and grateful attitude.

## weekly intentions

my top "go get-'em's" (fixes) to implement this coming week include:

incomplete action items, that support my goals, to carry over into this coming week include: (schedule them now and be specific.)

new action items, that support my goals, for this coming week include: (schedule them now and be specific.)

something new I'm grateful for this week, and with whom I will share it:

# When was the last time you sat on Santa's lap and told him what you wanted for Christmas?

Sitting on Santa's lap is only reserved for kids, right? WRONG! It's not just kids who dream big and fantasize about lofty adventures of what could be. We can all learn a little by letting our minds wander into the realm of the limitless. Who/what was it that put the damper on your dreams? Life, circumstances, family or so-called friends? Sorry, wrong again ... almost always, it's ourselves! It's time to stop blaming others and *believe*. It's time to chart the course toward our vision of greatness. Dig deep, tap into your desire and well of courage, and prepare yourself for some hard work. So, go on, indulge ... dream big and shout it from the mountaintops. *Which of your dreams could be resurrected by some hopeful holiday spirit?*

## reflections and intentions

my thoughts and feelings on today's FLASHPOINTS include:

my intentions and action items today include:

today I am grateful for:

# Differentiate, or die.

What makes you (and your organization) any different from the millions of others out there? While that sounded a touch more judgmental than I was hoping, it's an important question. Our competition is on the prowl, and they're wondering the same thing: How am I going to achieve success amongst the fog of products and services available? The answer: Zero in on what we love and what we're doing really well, and identify a client base who appreciates, wants (not needs), and will pay for it. That convergence is our angle. And when defining our value proposition, don't overlook the power of personality (ours), and those elements of our business or leadership style that uniquely define us. *Where have you innovated or differentiated, thereby avoiding the slow death of irrelevance?*

## reflections and intentions

my thoughts and feelings on today's FLASHPOINTS include:

my intentions and action items today include:

today I am grateful for:

# Nothing feels as lonely as being alone.

Being the high-achiever in any venture can get lonely at times, particularly when no one exactly understands our day-to-day responsibilities. Here's a fact: there are others out there who feel lonely, too. See, we're really not alone after all. Apart from networking and surrounding ourselves with other like-minded spirits who feel the same pain, seeking a mentor could be the ticket to greatness and the antidote to isolation. A good mentor has walked the same road before you, they know what it's like to search for solutions rather than to dwell on problems, and they'll keep us company when we're "in the weeds" and unable to turn to teammates for support. So STOP being lonely alone! *What do you need to do to get yourself some company?*

## reflections and intentions

my thoughts and feelings on today's FLASHPOINTS include:

my intentions and action items today include:

today I am grateful for:

# The truth hurts:
# Every worthy goal requires
# sacrifice, suffering and struggle.

Experienced leaders accept that saying "no" or "not now" to family and friends because of a project crisis is a necessary evil from time to time. Sadly, some wear their no's, their sleepless nights and their neglected health as a badge of honor, rather than accepting them as self-inflicted wounds due to a broken leadership model. I wish I could tell you that things will get easier or that you'll find your own work/life nirvana. Here's the truth: most leaders and entrepreneurs leave a trail of broken personal relationships; however, it need not be so. Real sacrifice comes from hard work spent protecting and prioritizing personal relationships and obligations against the revolving door of business and project crisis. *Where are ill-placed priorities affecting your personal and professional well-being?*

## reflections and intentions

my thoughts and feelings on today's FLASHPOINTS include:

my intentions and action items today include:

today I am grateful for:

> # Harmony is not the *lack* of conflict, but the *existence* of *inspired* and *innovative* options for responding to conflict.

A difference of opinions is no need for conflict...it simply means there is more than one point or view to be considered. Sure, it's true that coming to a unanimous agreement across the boardroom table can have a positive impact on workplace morale. It's also true, though, that a different opinion can lead to critical thinking, breakthrough ideas, and a discovery of passion! Wouldn't you rather embrace the discussions and exchange of new ideas that come from having diverse options on your team? It not only makes great business sense, but it's a great way to create an inclusive and tolerant business environment...the rewards of which are happier and more productive team members. *What's your relationship with inclusivity and diverging options?*

## reflections and intentions

my thoughts and feelings on today's FLASHPOINTS include:

my intentions and action items today include:

today I am grateful for:

> ## *People often say that motivation doesn't last. Well, neither does bathing; that's why we recommend it daily.*
>
> ### ~ Zig Ziglar

After five days of prompting and prodding new ideas and thoughts to come to mind, today we review what we've discovered. It's time to take a peek back at our journaling, to review our thoughts, feelings, and action items; and see how well we did. After all, self-awareness is the key to initiate growth and realize lasting change.

## weekly reflection

reflecting on my thoughts, feelings and experiences from this past week, the top three that impacted me the most include:

my top "ta-da's" (successes) from this past week include:

my top "oh-no's" (disappointments) from this past week include:

my top "ah-ha's" (discoveries) from this past week include:

> # *Winners must learn to relish change with the same enthusiasm and energy that we have resisted it in the past.*
>
> ## ~ Tom Peters

The end of the week is the best time to plan for the coming week. And at this point, you've reviewed the previous week and can be prepared to make changes and take actions based on thought, not re-action. You want to keep your goals in mind always. So today is your opportunity to look at yesterday's Weekly Reflection and decide what you're going to do and when. It is most often small tweaks that will lead to great success, fueled by a positive and grateful attitude.

## weekly intentions

my top "go get-'em's" (fixes) to implement this coming week include:

incomplete action items, that support my goals, to carry over into this coming week include: (schedule them now and be specific.)

new action items, that support my goals, for this coming week include: (schedule them now and be specific.)

something new I'm grateful for this week, and with whom I will share it:

## There's no greater leverage than a compelling vision, and an inspired team to make it so.

If we don't believe in ourselves or in the people we work with, can we really call ourselves effective leaders? It takes guts to identify a need or shortcoming and then make the choice to improve in that area. It takes even more courage to openly share our vision and to bring together a powerful and purposeful team to conquer it. Let's slow down briefly and consider that confidence, vision, and authenticity are traits in leaders that people find attractive. And since people like to *be good* and *do good,* it's our responsibility to leverage that desire and communicate effectively to *do great things.* It's our belief in our team, and in their potential, that empowers and enables them to multiply our efforts and impact. *How inspired is your team?*

## reflections and intentions

my thoughts and feelings on today's FLASHPOINTS include:

my intentions and action items today include:

today I am grateful for:

# Life may not have meaning, but who we are and who we become does.

It's an old age adage that humans spend a lifetime searching for the meaning of life. I'm not sure about the theology or psychology behind that, but I do know the sooner we get clarity, the more fulfilled lives we'll lead. Where would we even begin? Well, it's really quite simple. Ask yourself, "What are the things that I'm great at doing? What is it that I love to do? Of those things, which are most important to me?" And there's the list of priorities—the things that make us the happiest and are most important to us. Delegate, defer, or delete as much as possible from life that's not on the new priorities list. *Now is the time to stop searching and to start living. How will you prioritize?*

## reflections and intentions

my thoughts and feelings on today's FLASHPOINTS include:

my intentions and action items today include:

today I am grateful for:

# Remember this:
# All lies are told out of fear;
# the most evil are the ones we tell ourselves.

Remember that feeling of just having told a lie as a child? The insecurity, wondering if anyone will find out, and negotiating with ourselves about why it's okay to have lied. Some lies we forget all about, and others we remember years later (and sometimes the tinge of guilt still lingers). While it's one thing to tell a small lie as a child, it's neither useful nor acceptable as an adult to lie to others or ourselves. Sure, we all do it, but it's a slippery slope! Lies and half-truths are damaging to our reputation, and worse still, they zap our energy and wear away at our conscience, which leads to disease and pain. *How true are you to your own core values and to the people in your charge?*

## reflections and intentions

my thoughts and feelings on today's FLASHPOINTS include:

my intentions and action items today include:

today I am grateful for:

# Vision:
# Your ability to imagine
# a future greater than the present.

Having a clearly articulated vision for our lives and endeavors is critically important for a multitude of reasons; chief among them is the ability to inspire others and to create positive change in our communities. But what does it really mean to have vision? Close your eyes and imagine the look and feel of your world when your energy and efforts have served their ultimate purpose … this is your vision. It's much bigger than words printed on stationery or a clever sign hung in the break room. The real test of an articulated vision is whether our team and supporters understand what it takes to bring it to life, and whether they're equipped to take action to make it so. *What's needed to bring your vision to reality?*

## reflections and intentions

my thoughts and feelings on today's FLASHPOINTS include:

my intentions and action items today include:

today I am grateful for:

## 4th graders look like gods to 1st graders.

Jim Rohn famously said, "You are the average of the five people you spend the most time with." When we spend time with people who are more successful, experienced and talented than ourselves, we stand a chance to have some of that rub off on us. The same holds true for those dour, pessimistic naysayers nipping at our heels. All the way back to our childhood, we've learned from those with more experience: parents, teachers, tutors and even our classmates. Why change what works? Seek out opportunities to meet folks who are farther down the path, ask your role model for a moment of their time to discuss your ideas, even seek to learn from your own team members who have specialized skills. *Who are you spending time with today?*

## reflections and intentions

my thoughts and feelings on today's FLASHPOINTS include:

my intentions and action items today include:

today I am grateful for:

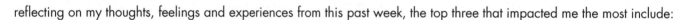

*Confidence is going after Moby Dick in a rowboat and taking the tartar sauce with you.*

~ Zig Ziglar

After five days of prompting and prodding new ideas and thoughts to come to mind, today we review what we've discovered. It's time to take a peek back at our journaling, to review our thoughts, feelings, and action items; and see how well we did. After all, self-awareness is the key to initiate growth and realize lasting change.

## weekly reflection

reflecting on my thoughts, feelings and experiences from this past week, the top three that impacted me the most include:

my top "ta-da's" (successes) from this past week include:

my top "oh-no's" (disappointments) from this past week include:

my top "ah-ha's" (discoveries) from this past week include:

> ## *Wisdom is knowing when to speak your mind and when to mind your speech.*
>
> ### ~ Evangel

The end of the week is the best time to plan for the coming week. And at this point, you've reviewed the previous week and can be prepared to make changes and take actions based on thought, not re-action. You want to keep your goals in mind always. So today is your opportunity to look at yesterday's Weekly Reflection and decide what you're going to do and when. It is most often small tweaks that will lead to great success, fueled by a positive and grateful attitude.

## weekly intentions

my top "go get-'em's" (fixes) to implement this coming week include:

incomplete action items, that support my goals, to carry over into this coming week include: (schedule them now and be specific.)

new action items, that support my goals, for this coming week include: (schedule them now and be specific.)

something new I'm grateful for this week, and with whom I will share it:

## Breathe. It does a body good.
## (And it's a long-term winning strategy).

As super achievers, we tend to cram so many tasks into our calendar that we don't even take a restroom break unless it's scheduled. Stop doing that! This sort of irresponsible scheduling doesn't give us the opportunity to slow down and reflect on those important heart and head decisions that shape our future. Nor does it give us a chance to consistently turn out our best work. Taking just 30 seconds a few times a day to close our eyes and slowly pull in a few deep breaths will soften the edge and bring a sense of calm, clarity and centeredness. Breathe. Your mind, body and spirit will all thank you. *Where will you schedule a few minutes of peace and quiet into your day?*

## reflections and intentions

my thoughts and feelings on today's FLASHPOINTS include:

my intentions and action items today include:

today I am grateful for:

# After a hard-fought battle, there's no substitute for celebration of victory.

Everyone wants to be on a winning team. Great team morale, attracting interested and passionate new team members, creating roles people love, genuine teamwork, clear milestones that help guide us and our organization towards the goals – all of these things are products of celebration in the workspace – and all improve productivity and margins. Coming together to celebrate achievements in the workplace has clear benefits to the business, through the people involved. Too often, because winning is hard work, business picks up too quickly after a win… and before we know it, months have passed without recognition of everyone's hard work and contribution. Perhaps celebrating victories should be part of your plan from the beginning. *What plans do you have for success and celebration?*

## reflections and intentions

my thoughts and feelings on today's FLASHPOINTS include:

my intentions and action items today include:

today I am grateful for:

# High achievers started as high believers.

We talk a lot about reaching for our dreams and crafting a vision for success—but what's the fun in dreaming, if dreams don't come true? Listen up, doubters. They DO! Sure, it takes guts to dream big, but let's face it, the next step is the scariest. That is, trusting that if we chase after our dreams with gusto, that it'll all work out. So start with the easiest part: Dream BIG! Let's pinpoint what it is we want out of life. What do you see in your future? What excites you? There's one critical step we must not forget: have *complete* faith that somehow, some way, we *will* attain our dreams. No second thoughts, 100% belief. *Do you believe? Good! What one step will you take in that direction?*

## reflections and intentions

my thoughts and feelings on today's FLASHPOINTS include:

my intentions and action items today include:

today I am grateful for:

> ## If I had to kick the person most responsible for my problems, I couldn't sit down for a week!
> ~ Dwight L. Moody

After five days of prompting and prodding new ideas and thoughts to come to mind, today we review what we've discovered. It's time to take a peek back at our journaling, to review our thoughts, feelings, and action items; and see how well we did. After all, self-awareness is the key to initiate growth and realize lasting change.

## weekly reflection

reflecting on my thoughts, feelings and experiences from this past week, the top three that impacted me the most include:

my top "ta-da's" (successes) from this past week include:

my top "oh-no's" (disappointments) from this past week include:

my top "ah-ha's" (discoveries) from this past week include:

> ## *He who dares to teach must never cease to learn.*
> ### ~ Anonymous

The end of the week is the best time to plan for the coming week. And at this point, you've reviewed the previous week and can be prepared to make changes and take actions based on thought, not re-action. You want to keep your goals in mind always. So today is your opportunity to look at yesterday's Weekly Reflection and decide what you're going to do and when. It is most often small tweaks that will lead to great success, fueled by a positive and grateful attitude.

## weekly intentions

my top "go get-'em's" (fixes) to implement this coming week include:

incomplete action items, that support my goals, to carry over into this coming week include: (schedule them now and be specific.)

new action items, that support my goals, for this coming week include: (schedule them now and be specific.)

something new I'm grateful for this week, and with whom I will share it:

# Your choices may be the only biography people ever read about you.

Life is full of choices. Dream or do? Lead or follow? Speak up or shut up? Our everyday choices will form who we are and will frame how our friends, fans, family and foes will remember us. We must possess the courage to do the hard right, over the easy wrong. What's most profound is that we're the only one who'll ever *really* know whether we're content with the choices we've made. Consider this: every choice we make is an opportunity to show our true colors. Like it or not, people are watching our every move. Decision-making is our opportunity to step into our God-given potential by taking action and being honest with ourselves (and our loved ones) about the greatness we hope to achieve. *How will you be remembered?*

## reflections and intentions

my thoughts and feelings on today's FLASHPOINTS include:

my intentions and action items today include:

today I am grateful for:

## I prefer not allowing one door to close before another opens. I'd rather keep the door open, even if it's just slightly ajar.

Sometimes in me, there are definite beginnings and ends, but never when there's a genuine human connection involved. When it comes to relationships and expanding our spheres of influence (notice I did not say "network"), there is never a limit on how we can interact with people. Even when we move on from close-knit relationships, there's often the opportunity to keep that door open and revisit the relationship in the future. To have this freedom, we must remain in contact with our tribe; this could be as simple as sending a "hello, just thought of you" card, or email, or text. My advice: keep your doors ajar. *Whom can you quickly reconnect with today?*

## reflections and intentions

my thoughts and feelings on today's FLASHPOINTS include:

my intentions and action items today include:

today I am grateful for:

## Ready, Set, GROW!
## It really can be this simple.

Where should we expand? How fast? When's the best time? So many questions and considerations! Abraham Maslow said, "You will either step forward into growth or you will step back into safety." That's a great way to look at the growth of our professional and personal pursuits. If we lack courage to step forward, we're actually moving backward as the fast-paced world passes us by. If we're *really* committed to excellence and to expanding our horizons, we must decide that we *want* to grow … then we'll figure out the "how." Take refuge in knowing that no matter which direction we start in, should we misstep, we'll have opportunities to make course corrections along the way. Ready? Let's go! *What's the most significant area in which you want to grow?*

## reflections and intentions

my thoughts and feelings on today's FLASHPOINTS include:

my intentions and action items today include:

today I am grateful for:

# Organizations are like organisms. They're not immune to infections, disease and dysfunction.

When recruiting team members, do you consider how team dynamics may shift with the latest addition? While that decision may not mean life or death to individual team members, personality conflicts could mean life or death to our organization. *It's really that serious.* Consider these tips when introducing new key team members: (1) *Understand* what inspires the team, then reinforce it during seasons of growth. (2) *Inform* the team why a superstar was chosen over other candidates, to reinforce the positive attributes and expectations we hold for the team. (3) *Remind* each team member how they positively impact the success of the team. (4) *Make* course corrections by enlisting new members if recent recruits simply don't perform. *What will you change for your next recruit?*

## reflections and intentions

my thoughts and feelings on today's FLASHPOINTS include:

my intentions and action items today include:

today I am grateful for:

# Think positive.
# Wait, strike that.
# DO positive!

There is no doubt that positive *thinking* has its benefits! But just thinking positively doesn't get us far when the bills are due. In a world of action, innovation and being proactive to get the most out of our teams, careers and personal lives, it's time to think and do positive! Norman Vincent Peale didn't just think about "The Power of Positive Thinking," he actually *did* something and *wrote it!* Positive doing is what's needed to release our positive thoughts to the world. We must take that first step outside our current comfort zone to serve others. Until we take that step, we're only dreaming. Decide *now* to turn your positive thinking into bold, consistent action. *What positive thought will you turn into action today?*

## reflections and intentions

my thoughts and feelings on today's FLASHPOINTS include:

my intentions and action items today include:

today I am grateful for:

> ## When you're feeling your worst, that's when you get to know yourself the best.
>
> ~ Leslie Grossman

After five days of prompting and prodding new ideas and thoughts to come to mind, today we review what we've discovered. It's time to take a peek back at our journaling, to review our thoughts, feelings, and action items; and see how well we did. After all, self-awareness is the key to initiate growth and realize lasting change.

## weekly reflection

reflecting on my thoughts, feelings and experiences from this past week, the top three that impacted me the most include:

my top "ta-da's" (successes) from this past week include:

my top "oh-no's" (disappointments) from this past week include:

my top "ah-ha's" (discoveries) from this past week include:

> ## The way to love anything is to realize that it might be lost.
> ~ G.K. Chesterton

The end of the week is the best time to plan for the coming week. And at this point, you've reviewed the previous week and can be prepared to make changes and take actions based on thought, not re-action. You want to keep your goals in mind always. So today is your opportunity to look at yesterday's Weekly Reflection and decide what you're going to do and when. It is most often small tweaks that will lead to great success, fueled by a positive and grateful attitude.

## weekly intentions

my top "go get-'em's" (fixes) to implement this coming week include:

incomplete action items, that support my goals, to carry over into this coming week include: (schedule them now and be specific.)

new action items, that support my goals, for this coming week include: (schedule them now and be specific.)

something new I'm grateful for this week, and with whom I will share it:

CPSIA information can be obtained
at www.ICGtesting.com
Printed in the USA
FSOW04n1744120617
35039FS